AIR
OPERATIONS

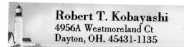

abc AIRPORT OPERATIONS
R.D. Palmer

Lufthansa

Oberhausen Europa Jet 727

LONDON

IAN ALLAN LTD

First published 1989

ISBN 0 7110 1823 5

Published by Ian Allan Ltd, Shepperton, Surrey; and printed by Ian Allan Printing Ltd at their works at Coombelands in Runnymede, England

Front cover:
V953C Merchantman G-APEM *Agamemnon* seen at East Midlands airport in 1988. The aircraft is operated by Air Bridge Carriers Ltd — Europe's largest all-cargo airline — on behalf of Elan International which offers an express parcels service with guaranteed next day delivery to selected European destinations. *B. Blanchard*

Acknowledgements

I have received invaluable assistance from many areas during the preparation of this book, particularly from airlines, airport operators and the manufacturers of airport equipment.

Particular mention must be made of the patience shown by David Ellis and David Farrell at Luton International Airport, Noel Rogers at Air BP International, Bruce Hales-Dutton of British Airports Services and Hiram Hardy of Monarch Aircraft Engineering. British Airways AERAD has also been particularly helpful with the reproduction of its aeronautical charts within the text.

Other companies and organisations which have kindly supplied photographs and details of their activities include: Avialift Products, Birmingham International Airport, British Airways, Civil Aviation Authority, County Tractors, Dan-Air, East Midlands International Airport, Edbro, Electric Vehicles Association, Epoxy Products, Esso Petroleum, F. L. Douglas (Equipment), Fluid Transfer, Garrett GmbH, Gatwick Airport, GEC Electrical Projects, Gloster Saro, Harbilt Electric Vehicles, Heathrow Airport, HeavyLift Cargo Airlines, Houchin, Land Rover, Locomotors, London City Airport, Manchester Airport, Reliance-Mercury, Reynolds-Boughton (Devon), Rolba, Saab-Scania, Scania (Great Britain), Schmidt Manufacturing and Equipment (UK), Simon-Gala, Smiths Electric Vehicles, Stonefield Vehicles, Transport Engineering, Vaisala (UK).

Finally, my thanks are especially due to my wife, Margaret, for her constant help and encouragement.

Contents

Introduction 6

1 General Features 9
Airport location, the anatomy of an airport, an airport at work

2 Passenger Operations 36
Terminal facilities, security, customs, cabin servicing, boarding, facilities for disabled passengers, VIPs

3 Cargo Operations 49
Parcels, mail, cargo, livestock, special cargo

4 Apron Technical Services 60
Power supplies, refuelling, minor maintenance, engine starting, pushback

5 Aircraft Maintenance 75
Legislation, inspection, servicing and maintenance, hangars

6 Airport Security and Emergency Services 86
Security, rescue and fire fighting equipment and operations, medical services, the system in action

7 Airport Navigation Services 99
Control tower, radar, radio and telecommunications, landing aids, lighting, meteorological equipment

8 Airport Maintenance 116
Patrols, birdstrike prevention, grass cutting, runway cleaning, runway repairs, winter operations, aircraft recovery

Glossary 128

Introduction

Airports: very few people are indifferent to them. For the business traveller they are a necessary evil, a potential cause for delay and frustration. For the holiday-maker they often represent the start of a break from workaday cares for a few weeks, whilst to some who live near them, airports can be a source of nuisance.

Love them or hate them, airports are now an essential part of the man-made environment, providing an interface between land and air. But having said that, all an aircraft needs to land on is a strip of ground long enough and strong enough for it to brake along, so why is a modern airport the size of a town? A lot of activity is there for all to see; for instance the ubiquitous shops and cafés, but there is far more going on, and often far from the public gaze.

As passengers sit in their aircraft at the end of the runway, and feel it shudder as thrust increases ready for take-off, they will often not spare a thought for the number of people intimately concerned with their safety at that moment. That is, of course, just how it should be — air traffic controllers, airport firemen, main-tenance engineers, or any of the dozens of other skills involved, their whole purpose in life is to ensure that civil air transport functions with absolute safety and lack of drama.

All airports which are used by civil transport aircraft must be so authorised by the issue of an Aerodrome Licence (Public Use). The conditions of this licence are extremely detailed, and cover all aspects of operation, with particular emphasis being placed on safety. The Civil Aviation Authority (CAA) is the body responsible for applying the licensing procedure in the UK, in the same way as it regulates all other aspects of civil avi-ation. The conditions of the Aerodrome Licence are, however, mainly uniform with international conditions imposed by the International Civil Aviation Organis-ation (ICAO), a United Nations body formed by the Chicago Convention of 1944. Formed as a permanent organis-ation in 1947, it now has its headquarters in Montreal and is responsible for the co-ordination and regulation of inter-national air transport.

As the UK embodiment of the ICAO, the CAA has wide powers over air transport and airport operators, covering such areas as financial standing and repute of operators (these could have an effect on safety), along with the provision of equipment deemed necessary for the safe and efficient handling of commercial aircraft. This equipment includes such items as navigational aids, lighting and emergency appliances. The CAA regu-lations go further by specifying how this equipment should be maintained and, in the case of rescue equipment, manned.

A further, and very important, con-straint imposed by the CAA concerns the location of an airport, and its effect on the surrounding area. This is not only to protect air passengers but to safeguard those who live and work in the environs of the airport. Most UK airports give the impression of having been built in the middle of a suburban sprawl, but in fact this is not the case because they were built either as RAF airfields or prewar commercial operations. When, in the early 1950s, civil aviation got back into its stride following World War 2, a pair of events conspired to bring airports, pre-viously isolated on the outskirts of towns, into the centre of built-up areas. The first of these events was the need to develop new housing, both to replace war damage in city centres and to meet the needs created by new public aspirations. The second event was the growth of airports as major industrial centres and communi-ties in their own right.

The sector of industry drawn to airports at first was that concerned with the business of aviation itself. A drive around the perimeter road at Heathrow Airport will reveal the premises of many companies engaged in the aviation industry, a situation repeated at airports all over the country. As a consequence of this there arose the need for housing in the area, as car ownership was low at the time (the workforce for these companies needed to live within easy commuting distance of their work).

Another group of employers to move to airport areas were the multi-national companies, to whom a site with good communications was more important than a city centre site, especially as city centres were becoming prohibitively expensive. Hard on their heels came new industries in fields which supported these organisations, fields such as electronics, which have now outgrown their origins and, to a large extent, diversified. Finally, the very size of airports themselves has become a magnet for development. About 47,000 people work at Heathrow, equivalent to the population of some towns, many of these people living in the immediate area of the airport.

One of the primary impacts of an airport upon its environment is noise. The problem was probably at its worst immediately before the widespread introduction of turbofan engines, which surround the hot exhaust stream with a shroud of cool by-pass air, rendering them much quieter than their turbojet counterparts. Although individual aircraft are now quieter, the number of air traffic movements (ATMs) is ever increasing, so the aggregate nuisance remains.

For this reason, all airports have a statutory duty to do all in their power to lessen the impact of noise upon their surrounding areas. The government places restrictions on the number of flights using the London airports largely as a result of noise, these restrictions encompassing such activities as night flying and determining arrival and departure routes so as to avoid populated areas. This latter results in the famous 'noise-abatement procedures' which necessitate a steep initial climb on full power followed by a reduction in power — and noise — when traversing areas of housing. The introduction of significantly quieter aircraft, such as the BAe 146, is allowing greater flexibility to airline and airport operators, because these transports can often operate below the noise threshold value for night operations.

Further to these powers, the government can also distribute air traffic between airports in a particular area, for example. Since 1986 there has been a virtual freeze on the number of flights using Heathrow, new services being directed into other airports in the south-east. Similar regulations forbid trans-Atlantic flights from any Scottish airport except Prestwick. Besides controlling the effects of airport operations on the environment, these regulations are used positively to promote the growth of particular airports. The ownership of UK airports underwent a major change with the introduction of the provisions of the Airports Act of 1986. The main provisions of this Act affected the structure of airport authorities; the most public result has been the transfer of the British Airports Authority from the public sector to form BAA PLC.

The British Airports Authority was formed in 1966 as a result of the Airports Authority Act of 1965. At that time it took control of Heathrow, Gatwick, Stansted and Prestwick from the government, followed by Edinburgh in 1971 and Aberdeen with Glasgow in 1975. Besides operating some of the world's busiest and most successful airports, BAA PLC, through its subsidiary British Airports Services Ltd, provides a very well respected consultancy service, working as an advisor to many overseas airports. Another subsidiary, British Airports International, provides a management service for airport authorities, including some in the UK.

The other main provision of the 1986 Act was the transfer of airports with a turnover of more than £1 million from local authority ownership to companies operating within the framework of the Companies Act. This has led to the financial restructuring of major regional airports such as Luton (in effect a London airport), East Midlands and Manchester, which has earned a reputation as an intercontinental airport.

Much of the traffic at these regional airports comes from charter holiday flights, but this brings problems in that such traffic is concentrated in the summer months — and then only at weekends. The result is facilities which are under-used during other periods. To help overcome this problem most airports are actively marketing themselves as — at least — business and feeder airports, feeding traffic into the international network. There is now a network of short-haul services operating in Britain, using aircraft such as the Shorts 330 or 360 to connect with major airlines at the south-eastern airports. Other airports, such as London City or Norwich, are marketing the claimed advantages of feeding into such airports as Paris or Amsterdam to connect with long-haul flights.

Fig 1   Examples of aircraft charges levied at London Heathrow airport

(All examples relate to aircraft undertaking international flights)

Boeing 747 — max take-off weight: 365,142kg with 450 passengers

	Peak charge	Off-peak charge
Navigation services	£299	£299
Landing charges	£290	£175
Passenger charges*	£4,972.50	£652.50
	£5,561.50	£1,126.50
Parking charges	£227.10/hr	£75.70/hr

Boeing 737 — max take-off weight: 53,070kg with 115 passengers

	Peak charge	Off-peak charge
Navigation services	£74.20	£74.20
Landing charges	£290	£175
Passenger charges*	£1,270.75	£166.75
	£1,634.95	£415.95
Parking charges	£58.62/hr	£19.54/hr

(charges correct at June 1988)

* Passenger charges are levied on each Terminal Departing Passenger, ie any passenger departing other than a transit passenger

Further charges could be raised for specialised services such as the supply of electric power etc

Information supplied by Heathrow Airport Ltd

Airport authorities derive revenue from both their aviation and non-aviation activities. Aviation-based revenue can come from the following sources:

● *Landing charges* — these vary with the weight of the aircraft being handled, and between peak and off-peak periods

● *Passenger charges* — levied on the number of passengers handled, again varying with time of day

● *Aircraft parking charges* — based on aircraft weight, length of stay and time of day

● *Specialised charges* — for services such as providing electric power and apron services

● *Revenue from non-aviation activities* — such as rent from shops and car parks has risen to the point where, at BAA airports, it now equals traffic revenue.

Aviation support services are provided from a variety of sources at UK airports; if an airline is strongly represented at an airport, the way British Airways is at Heathrow for instance, it may be economical to provide services such as apron handling, engineering support and cabin servicing for itself. If this course is chosen, the airline concerned will also provide these services to other carriers on an agency basis. Another option is for the airline to use the services of a company specialising in the ground handling of aircraft; companies of this sort are in attendance at most airports and have no affiliation to any airline; yet another method is for some facilities to be provided by the airport operator. There is no hard and fast rule as to the 'best' method, differing factors will determine how each airline and airport approaches the subject.

1 General Features

Airport location

No two airports are the same: a runway can comprise a strip of firm beach in the Scottish Isles, or a 4km ribbon of concrete at Heathrow. The differences occur because of differing operational requirements, history or geography. Despite these differences airports all fulfil the same purpose, so there are many universal features.

An airport has a voracious appetite for land — Heathrow has an area of 1,197 hectares (2,958 acres) for instance. That amount of land would be prohibitively expensive today, so airport development tends to be centred on existing facilities. There is, however, continuing talk of creating a totally new international airport some distance from London so as not to add to the air traffic congestion in the London Terminal Control Area, but well connected to the capital by surface transport. Some of Britain's modern airports are based on ex-military airfields, although examples of other types can be found such as at Luton and Southampton, both of which were built to serve adjoining aircraft factories. Both Liverpool and Gatwick, however, were built as civil airports from the outset.

An area of reasonably flat, firm land on which to build the main runway is the obvious requirement for a major airport. Although a slight gradient can be tolerated, the nearer that the runway is to dead level the better. Ideally, the environs of the airport should be free from hills so as to permit a long, shallow approach for incoming traffic. Where this is not possible, for instance at some Alpine airports, a price has to be paid in terms of the operating limits placed upon them. To complicate matters still further, the chosen site has to be well drained in order to support the massive foundations required for the runways, taxiways and aprons. With a wide-bodied jet tipping the scales at well over 350 tons the need for these foundations is apparent!

Many of the airports with RAF origins were laid out with their main runways at an angle to each other (Heathrow's famous 'Star of David' pattern is an example). This allowed aircraft to take-off and land with a minimum of crosswind, very necessary for a wartime bomber struggling into the air with a massive bombload, and scarcely less necessary for the civil transports of the immediate postwar period. With the coming of powerful, stable jet transports, the constraints relating to crosswind operation were eased, leading to many runways being either abandoned or relegated to taxiways. Those left in the UK have a largely western heading, to take advantage of the prevailing westerly wind in this part of the world.

An existing airport is allowed to object to planning applications for structures that might interfere with approach or departure routes, but the existence of such hazards would almost certainly lead to the refusal of a licence for a new airport, or the upgrading of an existing one. The CAA has comprehensive regulations governing the treatment of hazards to ensure that pilots can be certain that their routes to and from airports will be free of obstructions. The practical result of this is that any new international airport will need to be built on a 'green field' site, miles away from any city centre. An exception has been London City Airport, built on derelict land in London's docklands district to the east of the City. This airport is only able to operate owing to the STOL (short take-off and landing) capabilities of the four-turboprop de Havilland (Canada) Dash 7 airliner. The short field performance of this aircraft allows steep arrival and departure angles, clearing existing hazards that would preclude the airport's use by conventional aircraft. A future development could be the use of the four-turbofan BAe 146, but there is much local opposition to the use of larger-capacity aircraft than the Dash 7, although there is little difference in actual size or noise generation.

Given that any major international airport needs to be some distance from the city centre that it serves, it follows that good surface communications are essential. Good road links are an absolute necessity; Heathrow is served by the M3 and M4 motorways, and the M25 London orbital, although a journey on any of them in the vicinity of the airport is not for the faint-hearted! The London Underground's Piccadilly Line now operates into both the central area and Terminal 4, but is hardly suited to the carriage of international travellers owing to the limited baggage capacity available. The Underground also has a very valuable everyday function in helping to carry the army of airport workers. Although there are several plans to link Heathrow into the national railway system, many years are likely to pass before any of these becomes a reality, leaving Heathrow — the busiest international airport in the world — still connected to London by only the over-used M4.

The situation at Gatwick is better, as the airport has always boasted a main line railway station and which now offers four trains per hour. Birmingham International is similarly served with a half-hourly main line service. In addition, both airports are well served by road. The need for good rail links is now seen as so important that Stansted airport is being connected to the

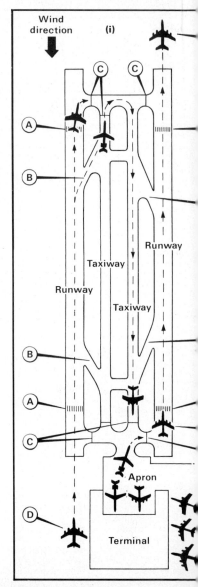

Fig 2 GROUND TRAFFIC FLOWS
(i) Airport With Parallel Runways

  A Thresholds
  B High-speed turnouts used by aircraft with shorter landing run
  C Taxiway holding points where aircraft wait for conflicting traffic to clear
  D Incoming flight
  E Outbound flight
  F Aircraft waiting for permission to take-off

(ii) Airport With Single Runway

  A Outgoing flight at taxiway holding point awaiting clearance of incoming aircraft

(iii) Airport With Main Entry Part-Way Along Single Runway

  A Aircraft waiting to take-off having backtracked from taxiway
  B Incoming flight taxiing back to apron

Liverpool Street/Cambridge line by a new tunnel into its terminal area, whilst plans are under discussion for Manchester airport to be rail-connected.

The Anatomy of an Airport

The most obvious feature of a major airport is the runway. It must be massively constructed to withstand the impact

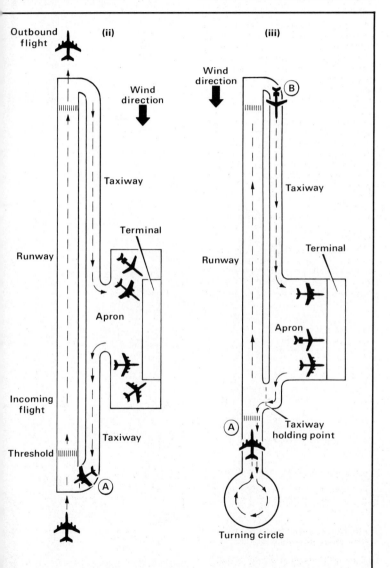

of loaded transports thumping down, day in, day out. Further to this the runway must be well-drained and have a high coefficient of friction to ensure safe braking for the aircraft using it.

UK airports are graded by the CAA into categories relating to the take-off distance, wingspan and undercarriage track of the largest aircraft using the facility. The resulting code determines the minimum runway width along with other criteria such as runway slope and sight lines. The lowest category is 1A, relating to aircraft with a wingspan of less than 15m and a take-off distance of less than 800m, whilst the highest, 4E, allows the use by aircraft with a wingspan of up to 60m and a take-off run of over 1,800m.

The main runway is constructed of several layers, the bottom one being a deep foundation, then two or more layers of concrete, and finally the actual runway

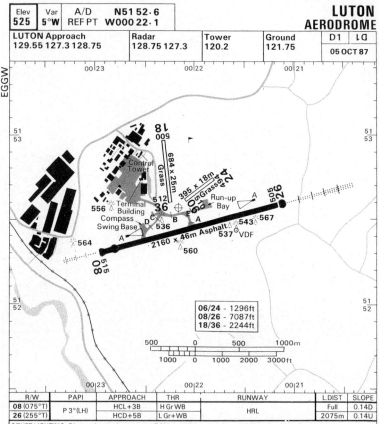

Fig 3 (above) Aerodrome chart for Luton airport — showing runway layout, dimensions, radio frequencies etc. *British Airways AERAD*

Fig 4 (right) Ramp chart for Luton — showing apron area in greater detail. *British Airways AERAD*

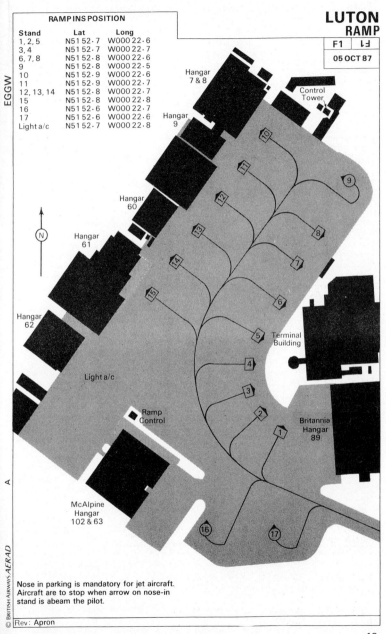

RAMP INS POSITION

Stand	Lat	Long
1, 2, 5	N51 52·7	W000 22·6
3, 4	N51 52·7	W000 22·7
6, 7, 8	N51 52·8	W000 22·6
9	N51 52·8	W000 22·5
10	N51 52·9	W000 22·6
11	N51 52·9	W000 22·7
12, 13, 14	N51 52·8	W000 22·7
15	N51 52·8	W000 22·8
16	N51 52·6	W000 22·7
17	N51 52·6	W000 22·6
Light a/c	N51 52·7	W000 22·8

Hangar 7 & 8

Control Tower

Hangar 9

Hangar 60

Hangar 61

N

Hangar 62

Light a/c

Terminal Building

Ramp Control

Britannia Hangar 89

McAlpine Hangar 102 & 63

Nose in parking is mandatory for jet aircraft.
Aircraft are to stop when arrow on nose-in
stand is abeam the pilot.

A

Rev: Apron

13

surface of either concrete or asphalt. Whatever the top surface, it must be grooved to assist in the drainage of surface water. This grooving is either applied before the surface has set, or will be cut into the hard surface by a series of diamond wheels.

The CAA lays down regulation areas surrounding the runway which must conform to certain characteristics. A stopway must be provided if the runway is long enough to permit take-off, but not an emergency stop following an engine failure during the take-off run. This stopway need not be of the same quality as the runway, but must be capable of bearing the weight of any aircraft using it, without causing or suffering damage. Many runways have sufficient length to permit an emergency stop within the paved area and therefore stopways are not required. Under all circumstances, however, the provision of a 'clearway' is necessary. This area, as its name suggests, must be cleared of any obstructions except those needed to assist air traffic, over which an aircraft can undertake its initial climb.

On either side of the runway and its stopway and/or clearway, extends the 'runway strip', an area which is also cleared of obstructions. It is intended to reduce the risk of damage to aircraft either running off the runway or flying low over it, for instance, during a missed approach. As with a stopway, a runway strip must be capable of taking the full weight of any aircraft using the runway. In the most stringent case, at a Category 3 or 4 airfield, this strip needs to extend at least 75m from the runway centreline. All lighting equipment, navaids etc within all the above areas must be frangible — that is so constructed that they break easily so as to cause the minimum of damage to an errant aircraft.

In addition to the above, some runways of less than 60m are required to have 'shoulders' — areas strengthened to withstand the blast from underslung engines.

Surrounding the runway can be seen the vast array of lights, radio antennae and navigational aids essential to the safe operation of modern air traffic. All these structures will be painted in as conspicuous a manner as possible, and have marker lights for use at night. As stated previously, all must break cleanly and easily if struck by an aircraft.

Main runways are identified by their magnetic heading, rounded to the nearest 10° and divided by 10. This number is painted on the downwind end of the runway. The number at the other end of the runway will always be a reciprocal (ie 180° different). Luton's main runway, therefore, is 26 when approached from the northeast, and 08 (260°-180°) from the other direction. Where two runways are parallel, they become L and R, left and right as seen from the approach.

From the main runways run the taxiways, providing passage to the aprons. Taxiways are the subject of special regulations in the same way as are runways. Their width, however, is significantly less owing to the lower speed of the aircraft using them. Taxiway strips, similar to runway strips, must again be provided.

After transitting the taxiways, the incoming aircraft reaches the apron. This must, like before, be extremely strong and stable, and large enough to accommodate with safety any aircraft likely to use it. Some idea of this size can be gained by imagining an oblong enclosing a 747; the area of this oblong will be over 45,000sq ft, or just over one acre! If possible, aircraft being parked for some time will be parked away from the active aprons, this reducing congestion and freeing expensive ground equipment for use by active aircraft. These parking areas are often a good distance away from the terminal and lack many of the features required for passenger handling. High-powered flood lighting is installed overlooking the apron to aid night operations, but this must be carefully designed so as not to cause confusion with navigational lighting, or project any glare upwards.

Adjoining the apron will be the passenger terminal buildings. There are currently different schools of thought about terminal design, although the architect is usually very limited in his solutions by what he has 'inherited' from previous architects and by the physical constraints of the site. Terminal buildings constructed in the immediate postwar period usually employ a long, straight airside frontage, with the departure and arrival gates being

Fig 5 (right)   Aerodrome chart for London Heathrow. *British Airways AERAD*

Elev 80	Var 5°W	INS RAMP	See chart F1

START & CLEARANCE HEATHROW Delivery 121.7	PUSH/TAXI Ground 121.9	TAKE-OFF Tower 118.7 118.5	ATIS 121.85	D1 LD 14 OCT 87

EGLL

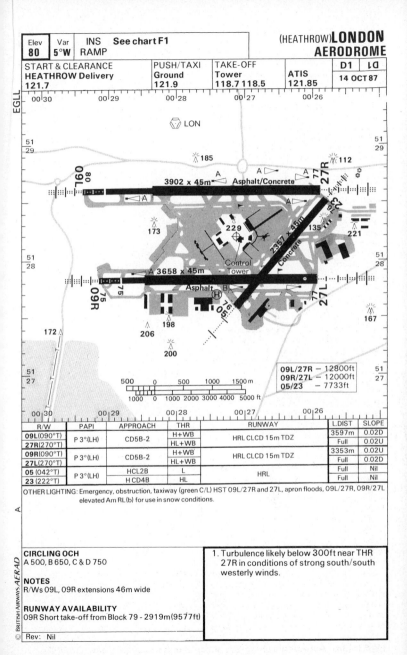

△ LON

3902 x 45m Asphalt/Concrete

160

2357 x 45m Concrete

229

Control Tower

A 3658 x 45m Asphalt

09R

27L

09L/27R — 12800ft
09R/27L — 12000ft
05/23 — 7733ft

R/W	PAPI	APPROACH	THR	RUNWAY	L.DIST	SLOPE
09L(090°T)	P 3°(LH)	CD5B-2	H+WB	HRL CLCD 15m TDZ	3597m	0.02D
27R(270°T)			HL+WB		Full	0.02U
09R(090°T)	P 3°(LH)	CD5B-2	H+WB	HRL CLCD 15m TDZ	3353m	0.02U
27L(270°T)			HL+WB		Full	0.02D
05 (042°T)	P 3°(LH)	HCL2B	L	HRL	Full	Nil
23 (222°T)		H CD4B	HL		Full	Nil

OTHER LIGHTING: Emergency, obstruction, taxiway (green C/L) HST 09L/27R and 27L, apron floods, 09L/27R, 09R/27L elevated Am RL(b) for use in snow conditions.

CIRCLING OCH
A 500, B 650, C & D 750

NOTES
R/Ws 09L, 09R extensions 46m wide

RUNWAY AVAILABILITY
09R Short take-off from Block 79 - 2919m(9577ft)

Rev: Nil

1. Turbulence likely below 300ft near THR 27R in conditions of strong south/south westerly winds.

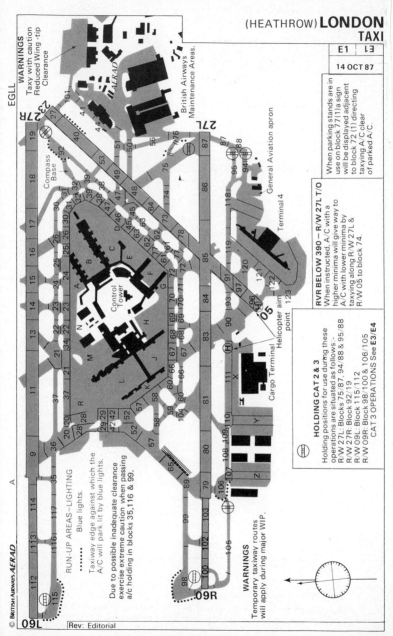

EGLL

WARNINGS
Taxy with caution
Reduced Wing-tip
Clearance

British Airways
Maintenance Areas.

General Aviation apron

Terminal 4

Compass
Base

Control
Tower

Cargo Terminal

Helicopter aim
point

RUN-UP AREAS – LIGHTING
Blue lights.

Taxiway edge against which the
A/C will park lit by blue lights.

Due to possible inadequate clearance
exercise extreme caution when passing
a/c holding in blocks 35, 116 & 99.

WARNINGS
Temporary taxiway routes
will apply during major WIP.

When parking stands are in
use on block 77 (1) a sign
will be displayed adjacent
to block 72 (1) directing
taxiing A/C clear
of parked A/C.

RVR BELOW 390 – R/W 27L T/O
When instructed, A/C with a
higher minima will give way to
A/C with lower minima by
taxiing along R/W 27L &
R/W 05 to block 74.

HOLDING CAT 2 & 3
Holding positions for use during these
operations are situated as follows :-
R/W 27L: Blocks 75/87, 94/88 & 95/88
R/W 27R: Block 92/19
R/W 09L: Block 115/112
R/W 09R: Block 98/100 & 106/105
CAT 3 OPERATIONS See **E3/E4**

© BRITISH AIRWAYS AERAD

Rev: Editorial

16

Fig 7 (below) Pier terminal system

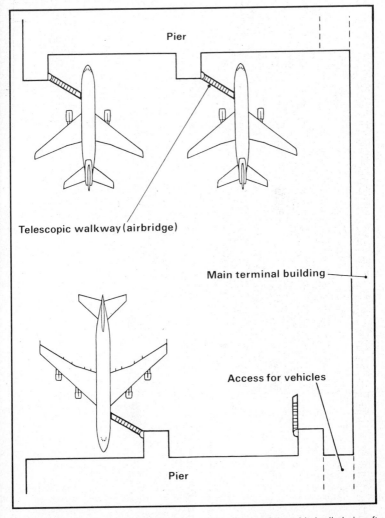

arranged along it. Whilst this was fine for small aircraft and moderate passenger volumes (conditions which still apply to many regional airports) different answers had to be found for the major undertakings.

The advent of the wide-bodied aircraft led to a radical rethink on terminal facilities. Existing designs would allow too few of the new transports to use them, whilst passengers would need to go on a route march to reach their boarding gates.

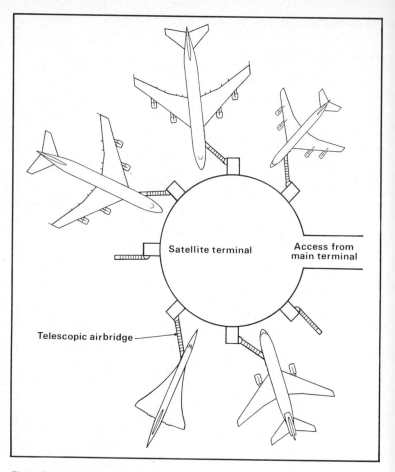

Fig 8 Satellite terminal system

The solution to both these problems was to build outwards, using part of the apron. The airside area so used was compensated for by more efficient docking practices; instead of rolling through on to a taxiway, aircraft would now nose-in to the terminal building and be pushed back after being reloaded. The distance walked by passengers could be reduced and covered telescopic walkways, known as airbridges, allowed passengers to leave and board their flights direct from the first floor of the terminal.

Two different broad styles of terminal are in use, depending largely on local conditions. With the pier system piers are built out into the airport leading to a series of aprons along either side, rather similar to some yachting marinas. Airbridges are installed at each stand, connecting the aircraft to the first floor lounge area. The ground floor is occupied

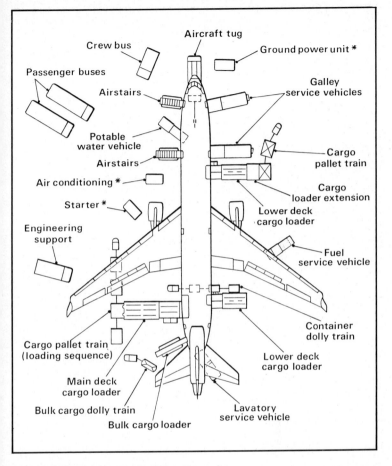

Fig 9 Vehicles involved in aircraft turnround

* Equipment not required when APU or ground mains are in use

by the baggage handling area, offices and other operational functions, whilst a service road runs along the face of the main terminal block linking the individual aprons.

The second layout is the satellite system. With this layout aircraft dock against a circular or polygonal terminal, once again utilising telescopic airbridges. The shape of these structures allows for easier manoeuvrability as each parking area tends to be wedge-shaped, but they cannot be linked to the main terminal in a conventional manner as only a narrow corridor is used in order to maximise apron space. The problem has been solved at Gatwick by connecting both the Satellite and the new North Terminal to the main terminal building by an automatic railway. Allied to moving walkways this means that passengers can reach their flights with a minimum of walking.

Within any airport terminal complex there is now the equivalent of a small town with shops, banks, bars and all manner of facilities in addition to the check-in desks, customs positions etc. These facilities, such as duty-free shops, are nearly always operated by a tenant company, rather than the airport owner. So important is the revenue from the leases of these units that, in the case of airports owned by BAA, they subsidise the airside activity to a substantial extent. Also to be found will be a health centre where, besides providing first-aid, the staff will be able to administer vaccinations if required. The staff are, of course, core members of the airport's emergency team.

Much in evidence will be the flight arrivals and departures boards, with the master display using either dot-matrix or flip-over displays. Backing these up will be numerous television monitors repeating the most urgent information. These displays, along with the public address system, are updated automatically by data fed from a computer system which in turn is driven by the air traffic control system. One of the systems at Heathrow controls all the displays, whilst allocating stands and preparing accounts for landing and parking charges at the same time. Another system, similar to a private teletext service, is transmitted to subscribers around the airport and contains page after page of information ranging from flight details to weather forecasts. As well as Heathrow's own staff, users include HM Customs, cargo agents and catering contractors.

Close to the terminal will be found the car parks, again usually operated by a contractor but contributing to the airport's revenue. Short-term parking will be nearest to the terminal for the benefit of 'meeters and greeters', whilst long-term parking will be some distance away, linked by a bus service. Taxi ranks and a bus terminal are to be found on the landside frontage of the air terminal building, along with access to the railway station where appropriate. Birmingham International Airport is linked to British Rail by a wheel-less train called the Maglev, which operates on the principle of magnetic levitation, whilst other locations where the distance is less use moving pavements.

Behind the scenes at the terminal will be suites of offices concerned with the more specialised aspects of air transport, such as the operations rooms where airlines will schedule crew and aircraft, customs offices and interview rooms, the meteorological briefing rooms where aircrew collect en route weather data which plays such a large part in the planning of the flight, and many more operations units.

Moving back airside, as the active area inside the security fence is known, we can see the cargo terminal some distance from the passenger aprons. This terminal will have its own apron similar in most operational ways to the passenger aprons but, naturally, of a more basic nature.

At all times and in all areas of the airport will be myriad road vehicles of all shapes and sizes. These have a multitude of functions concerned with all aspects of aviation support, be it aircraft maintenance or support of passenger and freight operations. One common feature shared by all airside vehicles is the amber obstruction beacon mounted on the highest point. This is switched on whenever the vehicle is operating in the company of moving aircraft, in order that the aircrew get maximum warning of the vehicle's presence. As an additional safeguard many vehicles are in radio contact with the control tower, and the drivers are obliged to seek authority before venturing outside closely defined areas. That notwithstanding, aircraft have absolute priority over vehicles owing to the very limited downward view from the flightdeck of most types.

An airport is a surprisingly hostile environment in which to operate road vehicles. Although distances covered are small, fuel consumption is high, owing to the time spent operating engine-driven equipment and crawling around in low gear. For this reason electric vehicles are becoming popular for airside use, but these have range limitations not shared by diesel-engined vehicles. Nothing is all things to all men! Clutch wear in diesel or petrol vehicles is so high because of the low operating speeds that many vehicles are specified with automatic transmission, thereby dispensing with the clutch in favour of a torque-converter. A second benefit is that, having an automatic gearbox, the driver of such a vehicle has more precise control — very desirable when inching around very expensive aircraft. Body damage is a real problem

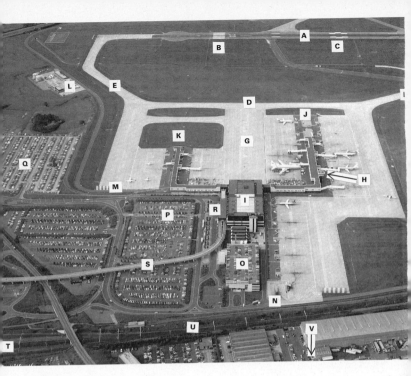

Above:
Birmingham International Airport from the air. *Birmingham International Airport*

Key

A	Runway 15/33
B	Threshold, runway 33
C	Touchdown Zone, runway 33
D	Taxiway 3
E	Taxiway 4
F	Taxiway 5
G	Apron
H	Control Tower
I	Passenger Terminal
J	International Pier
K	Domestic Pier
L	Fuel Tank Farm
M	Blast Fences
N	Security Control Gate, restricting access to airside areas
O	Multi-Storey Car Park
P	Shot-Term Car Park
Q	Long-Term Car Park
R	Main Entrance to Terminal
S	MAGLEV elevated railway linking British Rail station to passenger terminal
T	Birmingham International railway station
U	British Rail (London Midland Region) London-Birmingham main line
V	National Exhibition Centre

Top:
Lufthansa Boeing 727 rolling to a halt at Heathrow's Terminal 2. To the left is the airbridge, retracted to allow clearance for the incoming aircraft. *Jonathan Falconer*

Above:
Air Canada TriStar at Manchester Airport. In the background are Boeing 747s of British Airways and Singapore Airlines. The terminal shown is an interesting combination of pier and satellite systems. *Manchester Airport*

Right:
Air France Boeing 737-228 at rest on its stand. On the far side is the flexible canopy of the airbridge. The aircraft is drawing electric power from the 400Hz ground supply via the cable connected above the nose landing gear bay. *Jonathan Falconer*

22

The Arrival of an Air Littoral Embraer EMB120 at Heathrow
All photos Author

Above left:
The aircraft turns on to its stand under the guidance of a ground marshaller, the guide vehicle in the foreground having brought it along the taxiway system.

Left:
The marshaller brings the Embraer to a stop.

Below left:
The baggage truck backs up whilst the self-propelled GPU is connected. In the background the cabin cleaning staff wait to move in.

Top:
A catering truck backs down as the airstairs are lowered.

Below:
Refuelling commences as the passengers disembark.

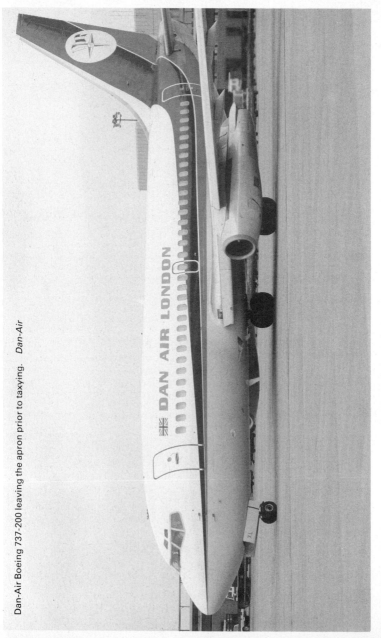

Dan-Air Boeing 737-200 leaving the apron prior to taxying. *Dan-Air*

with airside vehicles caused by the congested nature of their operating environment; whilst minor damage to the vehicle is an inconvenience, damage of any sort caused to an aircraft is potentially very expensive and, more importantly, dangerous. It is thus to be avoided at all costs. To conclude this chronicle of gloom we must consider tyre wear, which is very heavy because of the cocktail of spilt fuel and hydraulic fluid to be found on the ground; this mixture delights in eating rubber, so tyres have a short life and not a particularly happy one!

Buildings surrounding the apron are protected from damage by jet exhaust by either blast banks or fences, which serve to deflect and stream the noise and blast upwards away from the surrounding area. As an aside, aircraft with high-mounted engines such as the TriStar and DC-10 are forbidden from using their centre engine at anything above ground idle power whilst taxying because the efflux from these engines would miss the blast protection and cause damage.

An essential adjunct to any airport is the control tower, normally situated near the apron or above the terminal building. At the very top is the visual control room where a physical watch is kept on the airport and the surrounding sky, whilst at most busy airports there will be an approach control room on the floor below where a radar watch will be maintained. The control tower is, for obvious reasons, the highest building in the airport, offering an uninterrupted view.

The airport fire station is often near the tower at a small airport, but at larger airports will often be sited near the runways, or may be duplicated in order to meet the response times laid down by the CAA. The fire station will be similar to a local authority fire station, with an appliance hall enclosed by power-operated doors, accommodation for the crew to train and relax, and a watchroom. The watchroom is often in the form of a small control tower giving the duty watchkeeper a view of the runways, taxiways and aprons.

A major airport will be the centre of a web of electronic communication systems reaching, in some cases, right across the world. Telex links the controllers to air traffic control centres all over Britain and, via switching centres, to international facilities. Within the airport will be extensive private speech and data links to keep all operational staff in instant contact, especially in the case of an emergency, when these links will also be connected to outside emergency services.

Besides these fixed communications will be a range of radio telephone links, mainly air/ground radio but also ground/ground. The air/ground frequencies are used to communicate with the crew of aircraft at different phases of their approach or departure, as well as operations on the ground. Several ground/ground frequencies will be used to control the activities of vehicles airside, mainly for safety reasons, but also to direct airport service vehicles to where they are needed. Companies providing airside services may also operate their own radio systems, whilst the airport emergency services will be able to communicate with ground control, their own control and each other by means of radio telephone.

Having dwelt in some detail on the fabric of the airport, some mention must be made of the staff who make the whole thing work. The staff at any airport work for a variety of employers: of the 17,000 people at Gatwick, for instance, 1,300 are employed by the airport authority, whilst airlines employ 9,000. Engineering, fuel, catering and car parks are amongst the scores of other occupations represented which makes a large airport a microcosmic world of its own.

Many more will be working in the background in support of these people, looking after their health and safety in particular. Besides the usual risks associated with an intensive, highly-stressed occupation there are others particularly associated with working airside. The introduction of a new airliner with a shallow baggage hold, for example, has led to a crop of injured backs amongst loaders, whilst the introduction of 'strobe' anti-collision lights some years ago caused eye complaints amongst apron staff owing to the very bright output of these units.

In an environment as potentially dangerous as the apron, extra care must be taken by all concerned. Noise levels dictate that ear defenders are necessary in many areas and bright clothing is desirable as a passive safety measure amidst all the traffic weaving around. In all areas of aviation, however, safety has to become second nature.

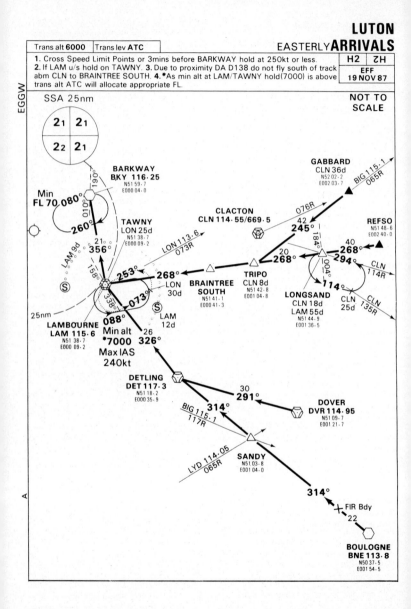

LUTON
EASTERLY ARRIVALS

Trans alt **6000**	Trans lev **ATC**		
		H2	ZH

1. Cross Speed Limit Points or 3mins before BARKWAY hold at 250kt or less.
2. If LAM u/s hold on TAWNY. 3. Due to proximity DA D138 do not fly south of track abm CLN to BRAINTREE SOUTH. 4.* As min alt at LAM/TAWNY hold(7000) is above trans alt ATC will allocate appropriate FL.

EFF 19 NOV 87

EGGW

SSA 25nm

2₁	2₁
2₂	2₁

NOT TO SCALE

BARKWAY
BKY 116·25
N51 59·7
E000 04·0

Min FL 70 080°
010°
260°

TAWNY
LON 25d
N51 38·7
E000 09·2
356°

CLACTON
CLN 114·55/669·5

GABBARD
CLN 36d
N52 02·2
E002 03·7
BIG 115·1
065R

076R
42 245°

REFSO
N51 48·6
E002 40·0
40 268°

LON 113·6
073R
253°
268°

268°
20 268°

294°
004°
CLN 114R

TRIPO
CLN 8d
N51 42·8
E001 04·8

BRAINTREE SOUTH
N51 41·3
E000 41·3

LON 30d

114°
LONGSAND
CLN 18d
LAM 55d
N51 44·9
E001 36·5

CLN 25d
CLN 135R

073°
338°
088°

25nm

LAMBOURNE
LAM 115·6
N51 38·7
E000 09·2

Min alt
*7000
Max IAS
240kt

LAM 12d

26
326°

DETLING
DET 117·3
N51 18·2
E000 35·9

30 291°

DOVER
DVR 114·95
N51 09·7
E001 21·7

BIG 115·1
117R
314°

LYD 114·05
065R

SANDY
N51 03·8
E001 04·0

314°

FIR Bdy
22

BOULOGNE
BNE 113·8
N50 37·5
E001 54·5

A

Fig 10 Easterly arrival routeings for Luton airport. *British Airways AERAD*

28

An Airport at Work

The first contact made by an incoming flight with its destination airport may well be many hundreds of miles before touchdown. The flightcrew will probably transmit on the 'company' frequency (ie, one outside the air traffic control network). This transmission will be to the airline's operations department and will report any defects that have occurred during the journey along with other details such as special requirements for passengers on the flight, for instance.

At the same time data regarding the flight's progress will be fed into the airport's information systems from the national air traffic control network, and this information disseminated to all interested parties. They will then use it to update their plans for dealing with the flight upon its arrival. In the case of an airport of the calibre of Heathrow, the information from the Air Traffic Control Centre (ATCC) will be fed into the airport's computer system and will be used to allocate a stand, warn the catering contractor and fuel supplier, and insert the flight into the arrivals displays in the terminal.

Back on the flightdeck of 'our' flight the aircraft will still be under the control of ATCC, but the crew will be selecting the relevant charts for their destination which may well have a Standard Arrival Route (STAR) procedure in operation. With these procedures the incoming flight follows a predetermined route, crossing various radio beacons and following their radials. This saves the chore of the controllers having to read individual routings over the air, thus saving valuable time. During this last part of the en-route phase of the flight the crew will be gathering the meteorological information for their impending landing; at smaller airports this will be read out by the controller whilst at busier airports this information is continuously broadcast by an automatic system known as Automated Terminal Information Service (ATIS). Altimeters are set to the local barometric pressure, using this information to save the acute embarrassment of finding the ground higher than one thought!

Each airport has a reporting point where control passes from ATCC to aerodrome control. At this point the radios will be switched to the frequency of the approach controller, the pilot will identify the flight (although approach will already be aware of its presence because of information from ATCC) and will confirm that they have the current ATIS bulletin. From here there are differences in the way the arrival is handled, depending on the size and traffic volume of the airport in question. We will assume, however, that we are landing at a large, busy airport.

The initial approach is made under the surveillance of the airport's approach radar, which not only shows the position of the flight in relation to other traffic and the runways, but also by means of Secondary Surveillance Radar (SSR) identifies the flight and displays its altitude alongside its trace on the radar screen. Our aircraft will at this point be either directed straight on to the extended line of the runway, or at busy times be instructed to join the top level of the holding pattern, commonly known as the 'stack'.

This holding pattern — Heathrow has four — involves incoming aircraft orbiting a VHF omni-range (VOR) beacon in a precise pattern, each aircraft following the same 'racetrack' pattern 1,000ft above the next lowest. As an aircraft reaches the lowest level it is called forward to start its approach. Each aircraft then descends 1,000ft thus leaving the top level free.

In either case the flight will proceed under the direction of the approach controller who will space aircraft along the approach path so as to ensure that each flight has time to vacate the runway before the next arrival. This separation is also important in avoiding aircraft being buffeted by the turbulence of the preceding flight; eight miles is needed behind a wide-bodied jet to allow the air to settle.

The approach controller will in some cases have other duties as well. At Heathrow, two incoming streams — one from the north and one from the south — need to be integrated into one stream of arrivals on the extended centreline. At an airport with only one main runway such as Gatwick, the arrival and departures need to be co-ordinated so that one slots in with the other.

At a distance of between six and eight miles the aircraft should have been settled on to its approach path by the approach controller, who will have placed it in its proper place in the sequence, and at its correct height and speed. Having done this he will hand over to the aerodrome controller. At a busy airport this function is sub-divided between the air arrivals controller and the ground movements controller. Both of these are situated in the glazed Visual Control Room (VCR) atop the tower.

The air arrivals controller issues permission to land, having satisfied himself that the runway and relevant airspace is clear, and will briefly confirm wind speed and direction. As well as an excellent field of view, he may have the assistance of a small radar display, called the Distance From Touchdown Indicator (DFTI), which just displays the section of the main plot which concerns the approach. This is used to inform him of the sequence of incoming flights.

By this time the pilot will have established the aircraft on the Instrument Landing System (ILS), and this will either provide guidance for him or actually fly the aircraft down the glideslope via the autopilot. The pilot will be instructed to report to the arrivals controller at the outer marker, a beacon about four miles from the threshold. The ILS will bring the aircraft down to a height where guidance can be received from the approach lighting. In some cases the ILS is developed into a full autoland system capable of guiding the aircraft on to the runway, in almost zero visibility.

After the aircraft has touched down the pilot will report the fact to the arrivals controller, who will inform him of the exit from the runway to take, and instruct him to re-tune to the frequency of the ground movements controller. The ground movements controller is responsible for the safe passage of the aircraft from the runway to the apron, besides regulating the movements of airside vehicles by means of a separate UHF radio channel. Some airports have the facility of Airfield-Surface Movement Indicator (ASMI), which is a high-speed, high-resolution radar which can depict all the ground movements going on, irrespective of the actual visibility.

Various concerns connected with the turning round of the flight will have received details of its stand number and estimated time of arrival from the airport computer system so, when the aircraft rolls into its stand, various resources will be awaiting its arrival, as if ready to pounce. The position of the plane on the stand is critical, especially if an airbridge is being used, so the pilot will be guided by either a ground marshaller using hand signals, or one of a variety of optical aids to alignment. As soon as the aircraft stops, chocks are wedged under the nosewheel and electrical power introduced, if necessary. The throttles will then be closed to stop the main engines.

While the engines spool down all hell appears to be let loose as the waiting throng descend on the aircraft. As the doors are opened, steps or airbridge will be moved into position, unless the aircraft carries its own airstairs. The passengers begin to disembark, baggage is unloaded from the belly hold ready to meet up with them at the carousel, whilst the caterers start to take the debris left from the in-flight meals and cleaners attack the cabin to ensure its cleanliness.

Any faults reported over the company radio will now be cleared, if possible, by the engineering staff, whilst others complete less obvious but essential tasks such as servicing the toilets. All this frantic activity is supervised by a ramp supervisor, one of his duties being to prevent a huge traffic jam building up by regulating the arrival of the various units involved by means of a pocket radio-telephone.

Meanwhile, the crew taking the aircraft on its next leg will be well on their way through their preparations, having filed their flight plan which inserts the flight into the air traffic control network. They will also scan the current Notices to Airmen (NOTAMS) which will tell them of such problems as navaids being out of commission, or runways being out of use at various airfields. They will pick up the en route and terminal weather details and the preliminary load sheet for the flight, and from these they will decide on the fuel to be taken on board for the flight.

The fuel order is given to the ground engineer who, in turn, will pass it on to the fuel company's operator. He will start loading the fuel under the supervision of the ground engineer. Whilst this happens, drinking water will be pumped aboard,

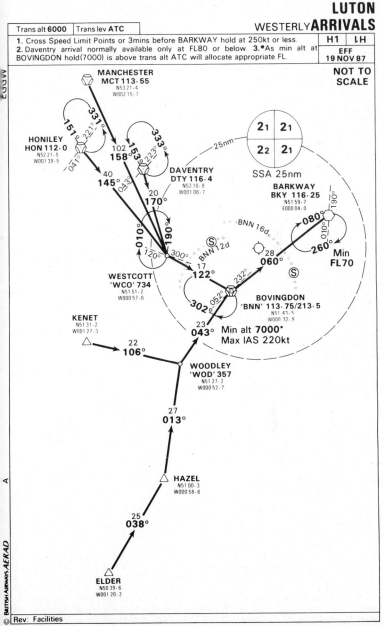

Trans alt **6000**	Trans lev **ATC**

1. Cross Speed Limit Points or 3mins before BARKWAY hold at 250kt or less.
2. Daventry arrival normally available only at FL80 or below. 3.*As min alt at BOVINGDON hold(7000) is above trans alt ATC will allocate appropriate FL.

H1	LH
EFF	
19 NOV 87	

NOT TO SCALE

MANCHESTER
MCT 113·55
N53 21·4
W002 15·7

HONILEY
HON 112·0
N52 21·5
W001 39·5

331° 151° 221° 041°
102 153° 223° 333°
158° 040°
40 **145°**
20 **170°**

DAVENTRY
DTY 116·4
N52 10·8
W001 06·7

010° **190°** 120° 300° **BNN 12d**

WESTCOTT
'WCO' 734
N51 51·2
W000 57·6

17 **122°** 232° 052° **060°** 28

302°

BARKWAY
BKY 116·25
N51 59·7
E000 04·0
190° 080° 010° **260°**
Min **FL70**

BNN 16d

SSA 25nm
| 2₁ | 2₁ |
| 2₂ | 2₁ |
25nm

BOVINGDON
'BNN' 113·75/213·5
N51 43·5
W000 32·9

23 **043°** Min alt **7000***
Max IAS 220kt

KENET
N51 31·2
W001 27·3
22 **106°**

WOODLEY
'WOD' 357
N51 27·2
W000 52·7

27 **013°**

HAZEL
N51 00·3
W000 58·6

25 **038°**

ELDER
N50 39·6
W001 20·2

Rev: Facilities

Fig 12 (right)   Easterly Standard Instrument Departures from Luton airport.
British Airways AERAD

the caterers will be loading food into the galleys, whilst the cabin crew prepare the cabin to receive the new passenger complement. Back on the stand, baggage and cargo is being loaded into the holds.

As the flight crew walk to the aircraft, either the pilot or (if one is carried) the flight engineer will check with the ground engineer on its state of health, including whether the work reported by the previous crew has been cleared. He will then walk around the aircraft on the apron, checking for fluid leaks, that no control surfaces have been damaged and that all access panels have been secured, amongst other things. This process is only a brief back-up to the work of the ground engineer, and is flippantly known as 'kicking the tyres', but is a valuable addition to the aircraft's safety audit.

The passengers will soon be boarding as the flight crew start to ready the flightdeck, selecting charts and setting the frequencies of the first navaids to be used on departure, whilst at some airports they will be able to consult a departure ATIS. Around this time the despatcher — who has been responsible for the boarding of passengers, baggage and cargo — will present the captain with the final load sheet. The take-off weight can be ascertained from this, and consequently the all-important take-off speeds calculated. The three critical speeds are:

- V^1 The maximum speed at which a take-off can be aborted safely following a loss of power.
- V^2 The minimum speed at which a safe take-off can be accomplished following the loss of power from one engine.
- V^R The speed at which the aircraft can be rotated (ie the nose lifted) to become airborne on a normal take-off.

If an Auxiliary Power Unit (APU) is provided aboard the aircraft this will now be started, and the electrical load transferred to it from external power which will then be disconnected. If, as in the case of older jets and turboprops, an APU is not fitted, external power will be provided until main engine start which will be accomplished with the help of an air start

unit. This unit will arrive on the apron at about the same time as the airtug, which will be coupled up to the nosewheel ready to pushback. The ground engineer will now plug the lead of his headset into a socket near the nose of the aircraft, enabling him to speak to the crew on the flightdeck.

The captain and first officer will now be running through their checks and, having ascertained that the cabin is secure, order the steps or airbridge away and all doors closed. After checking with the ground engineer that all doors and hatches are secure, he will radio for clearance to start main engines. This clearance will be given only if the flight can commence reasonably quickly. If any delay is foreseen — either at the airport, nationally or even internationally — the ground movements planner will withold permission to start, thereby saving fuel for the operator as well as reducing the risk of congesting the taxiways. However, if all is clear, start clearance will be given and the pilot instructed to change frequency to that of the ground movements controller. The anti-collision lights will be switched on to warn airside personnel to keep clear of engine intakes and exhausts, and permission to pushback obtained from the tower. The ground movements controller will satisfy himself that he is not setting any conflicting movements up, and that he is releasing aircraft on to the taxiway with sufficient separation. He will then authorise pushback.

After pushback, engine start will be completed and the engine pressure and temperature gauges scanned to ensure that all is within limits. The ground engineer will similarly have been watching each engine start, looking for the merest hint of any abnormality. Having satisfied themselves that all is functioning properly the flight crew will dismiss the tractor, and the ground engineer will disconnect his headset and walk away to the wingtip holding his headset jackplug aloft to prove to the pilot that it is free of the aircraft.

Taxi permission is obtained from the ground movement controller who will advise the pilot of his taxying route, and any points where he should hold and seek

EGGW

| Trans alt **6000** | | | | | | | | G1 | LG |

1. Initial climb: Ahead to 500(QFE). **2.** Max IAS 250kts below FL100 unless authorised.
3. En Route cruising level will be issued after take off by London Control. **4.** R/W 26 Min gradient 4.5% (270'/nm) to 200'aal.

05 OCT 87

G/S kt	100	130	160	190	220	250	
ft/min	450	590	720	860	990	1130	270'/nm

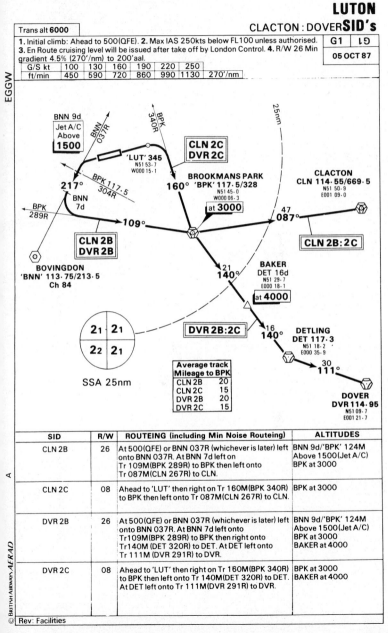

SID	R/W	ROUTEING (including Min Noise Routeing)	ALTITUDES
CLN 2B	26	At 500(QFE) or BNN 037R (whichever is later) left onto BNN 037R. At BNN 7d left on Tr 109M(BPK 289R) to BPK then left onto Tr 087M(CLN 267R) to CLN.	BNN 9d/'BPK' 124M Above 1500(Jet A/C) BPK at 3000
CLN 2C	08	Ahead to 'LUT' then right on Tr 160M(BPK 340R) to BPK then left onto Tr 087M(CLN 267R) to CLN.	BPK at 3000
DVR 2B	26	At 500(QFE) or BNN 037R (whichever is later) left onto BNN 037R. At BNN 7d left onto Tr109M(BPK 289R) to BPK then right onto Tr140M (DET 320R) to DET. At DET left onto Tr 111M (DVR 291R) to DVR.	BNN 9d/'BPK' 124M Above 1500(Jet A/C) BPK at 3000 BAKER at 4000
DVR 2C	08	Ahead to 'LUT' then right on Tr 160M(BPK 340R) to BPK then left onto Tr 140M(DET 320R) to DET. At DET left onto Tr 111M(DVR 291R) to DVR.	BPK at 3000 BAKER at 4000

© BRITISH AIRWAYS AERAD

Rev: Facilrties

Trans Alt **6000**		G2	ƧⅮ
		05 OCT 87	

EGGW

1. Initial climb: Ahead to 500(QFE). 2.**Report passing BNN 328R to ATC. 3. A/C unable to comply with SID's or non standard clearance must inform ATC prior to take off. 4. En Route cruising level will be issued after take off by London Control. 5. Max IAS 250kt below FL100 unless authorised. 6. R/W 26 Min gradient 4.5% (270'/nm) to 200'aal.

G/S kt	100	130	160	190	220	250	
ft/min	450	590	720	860	990	1130	270'/nm

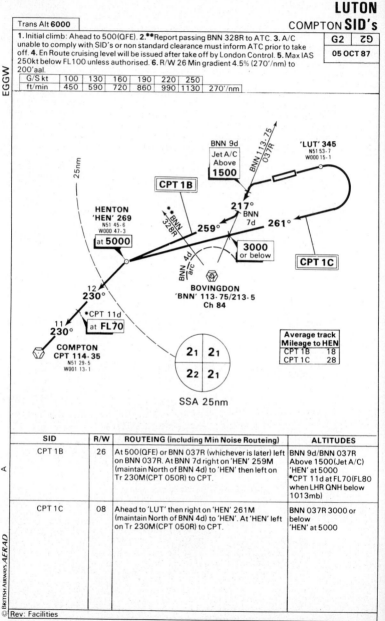

Average track Mileage to HEN
CPT 1B — 18
CPT 1C — 28

SSA 25nm

SID	R/W	ROUTEING (including Min Noise Routeing)	ALTITUDES
CPT 1B	26	At 500(QFE) or BNN 037R (whichever is later) left on BNN 037R. At BNN 7d right on 'HEN' 259M (maintain North of BNN 4d) to 'HEN' then left on Tr 230M(CPT 050R) to CPT.	BNN 9d/BNN 037R Above 1500(Jet A/C) 'HEN' at 5000 *CPT 11d at FL70(FL80 when LHR QNH below 1013mb)
CPT 1C	08	Ahead to 'LUT' then right on 'HEN' 261M (maintain North of BNN 4d) to 'HEN'. At 'HEN' left on Tr 230M(CPT 050R) to CPT.	BNN 037R 3000 or below 'HEN' at 5000

Rev: Facilities

further clearance. The flight will be slotted into the pattern of departing aircraft and the pilot told of his number in the queue. Whilst taxying, the crew will be running through further checks prior to take-off.

The take-off controller will take over during this phase, telling the pilot where to hold before turning on to the runway. Once at the head of the queue, the flight will be turned on to the runway and instructed to hold pending the previous flight being clear. When this happens, a brief check on wind direction and strength will be given and the pilot cleared to take-off. During the initial climb the pilot will be instructed to contact ATCC by the take-off controller who will end the airport's involvement with 'our' flight. It will now be proceeding along its Standard Instrument Departure (SID) route, in much the same manner as another flight is following its STAR, and establishing contact with approach control.

Below:
Dan-Air BAe146/100 starting its taxi run. *Dan-Air*

2 Passenger Operations

Terminal facilities

Even though airports now handle more and more freight, their primary function is still that of passenger handling. Different categories of traveller rightly expect different facilities from an airport; the business traveller will look for late check-in times, telephones and secretarial services perhaps, whilst the holidaymaker will probably be interested in gift shops, cafés and bars.

The modern passenger terminal building has developed to meet as many of these — often conflicting — needs as possible; indeed it often incorporates all the facilities of a small town. To many travellers, particularly those embarking on their holidays, an airport can be a confusing, exciting place where adrenalin starts to flow and, some would say, common sense starts its holiday too. For this reason much thought has been put into making airports as 'user-friendly' as possible with good, clear information displays and large, pleasant circulating areas where intending passengers can catch their breath whilst they await the departure of their flights.

Passengers are likely to arrive at an airport by a variety of means. Whatever their mode of transport, their first task will be to check-in with the airline which will relieve the travellers of their baggage, having weighed it, confirm details of flight time and departure gate, and issue a boarding pass. At this point the baggage is weighted, coded and dispatched on a conveyor belt. We shall see what happens to it later in this chapter.

The passenger is now free to fill in his or her time until their flight is paged, or shown on the departure display. Most airports now have a range of shops and eating places available, together with banks and post offices. As detailed in the last chapter, these establishments are managed by retail operators who pay rent to the airport authority, which in turn uses this very welcome revenue to help subsidise the primary, aviation-related aspects of its business. All the facilities in this part of the airport are still landside, however, so not free of national duties and taxes.

Security

For the passenger, the barrier between landside and airside is the entrance to the departure lounge from the main concourse, where initial security checks take place. These checks now carried out for both international and domestic flights, are to detect any firearms, weapons or explosives which could be used in a hijack attempt or terrorist act. The body search has now been superseded by an arch which the passenger walks through; this arch contains an electro-magnetic field, the pattern of which is disrupted by the presence of metallic objects within it. Hand luggage is X-rayed by low-power equipment which displays the contents of the bags on a screen. Equipment is also used which can detect the scent given off by explosives, either hidden in baggage or on clothing. Great care is taken by security organisations to guard against the effects of tedium causing a loss of concentration on the part of the operators; relatively short periods of duty are therefore necessary to ensure maximum alertness.

In addition to these universal checks, the international traveller will be subject to further scrutiny, passport control in particular. The main reason for checking the passports of outgoing travellers is to try and stop people wanted in connection with criminal activities from leaving the country. The officers engaged on passport control have details of those likely to attempt to flee and, if they suspect that such a person is before them, they can discreetly summon assistance.

For the incoming passenger, the emphasis is on trying to apprehend those endeavouring to enter the country illegally, either as illegal immigrants,

Fig 14 Departure flow chart

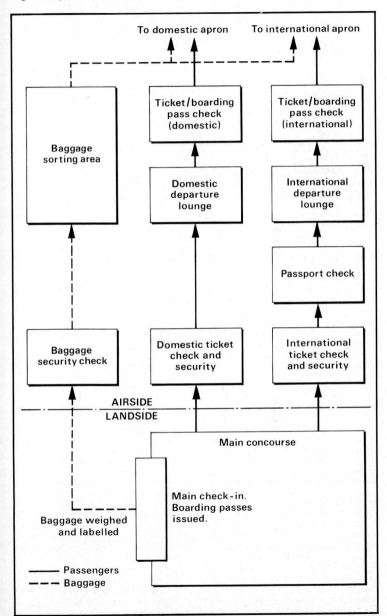

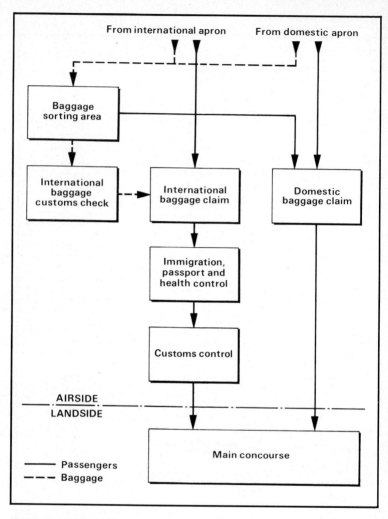

Fig 15 Arrival flow chart

smugglers, or those intending to take part in criminal activities during their stay. A further control is exercised on the health of passengers from certain parts of the world, and certificates may need to be produced to prove the currency of vaccinations, for instance.

It is sad that these measures look like being necessary for evermore, and that

the casual attitude displayed in some parts of the world can negate all the effort expended by the more responsible nations in the field of security.

Security is the very highest priority at any airport; recently this was highlighted by the officers patrolling Heathrow carrying semi-automatic weapons to enable them to respond to any threats more quickly. Much covert surveillance is used employing both closed-circuit television and plain clothes officers in discrete radio contact with their control room. Beside the risk of wrongdoers gaining access to the airside, security authorities are constantly alert for unwelcome visitors trying to enter the country. For this reason, passport and immigration control is no longer a formality, nor is customs control.

Customs

HM Customs and Excise is in the forefront of the dangerous business of stemming the flow of drugs into this country and many methods are used in this fight. International co-operation between anti-drug agencies is now commonplace, and often yields spectacular results; many large drug shipments are intercepted after intelligence is received from the country of departure. As well as through organised shipments such as this, large quantities of drugs also arrive by ad hoc couriers with amounts of illegal substances concealed about their person or in their baggage. These people are frequently apprehended after plain clothes customs officers, highly skilled in observing human nature, have noticed suspicious behaviour before the courier reaches the customs barrier.

Outgoing passengers, having cleared security, pass into the departure lounge. In the case of international flights, passengers are outside national customs regulations once they are airside, and this is the reason that duty-free shops are to be found in departure lounges of international airports. These shops are, once again, managed by retailers who pay rent to the airport authority, and they sell a wide variety of goods at reduced prices, owing to the absence of excise duty. There is much criticism of this sale of duty-free goods at the port of exit because it results in large quantities of liquor being flown as cabin luggage, with consequent fire risk and weight penalty. Customs authorities defend the practice on the grounds that duty-free goods can only be exported — if sold at the port of entry they would, in effect, be imports.

In 1992 the EEC intends to remove all customs barriers throughout the Community, but what effects this harmonisation will have remain to be seen. Security procedures will need to be amended once EEC residents are able to travel to Europe without restriction, whilst the abolition of duty-free sales could strike a blow against airport operators by removing the revenue from airside shop rents.

Cabin servicing

Whilst passengers scan the information displays in the departure lounge — perhaps taking a small, or not so small, duty free tincture to calm their nerves — the finishing touches are being put to the preparation of their aircraft ready for their embarkation.

Since its arrival much work will have been done to the aircraft, both to the passenger accommodation and to its systems. As soon as the previous passengers have disembarked, a small army of workers will have descended on the aircraft to start the intensive task of turnround. Amongst the first aboard will be the customs officers who will check the records concerning the sales from the bar, and then seal the remaining stock to prevent any duty free goods finding their way landside; at the same time the cleaning staff will begin to give the cabin a thorough grooming. Items such as headrest covers are changed, ashtrays emptied and upholstery and carpets vacuumed. Catering contractors will remove the remains of the previous flight's meals, rolling the meal trolleys from the galleys into their high-lift vehicles. Beneath the fuselage, the sanitation tanker — euphemistically called a 'honey cart' — is using its vacuum equipment to empty the cabin toilets and waste water tanks.

After the aircraft has been cleaned through, the task of re-provisioning for the next flight begins. Once again, beneath the aircraft clean water will be pumped aboard from a low-profile tanker mounted on a light goods chassis; to avoid mistakes this often carries the legend 'potable water' in large letters on its sides. The catering trucks will have returned to deliver the food for the next flight, replacing the containers removed earlier with full ones carrying meals, part-cooked in huge kitchens on the edge of the airport. Any special requirements — such as meals for people with special dietary needs, religious meals or meals for children — are prepared on the instructions of the airline which will have such details to hand from the passenger manifest. The cabin crew, meanwhile, will be checking the bar stock aboard, often replacing the partially full trolleys from the previous flight with full ones containing the complete bar imprest, again under customs seal.

The passengers' baggage will make its appearance on the apron about now, so a look at how it got there would be appropriate. When last seen by its owners this baggage was disappearing along a conveyor belt behind the check-in counter, where the ground steward or stewardess had affixed a ticket to the handle. This ticket identifies the flight involved to the baggage handlers working behind the scenes in the baggage handling area. The information contained on the ticket may be in simple alpha-numeric form, in which case the handler reads the flight number and sorts it manually, or it may be in the form of a barcode. This barcode, similar to those used on groceries, is scanned by a laser scanner which informs the sorting machinery which flight the bag is bound for; the conveyor then tips it off at the correct station for loading. Other sorting systems rely on a computer memory to keep track of the bag, its flight number being keyed in at the check-in desk.

In the handling area the bags are loaded — either into containers or loose — on to trolleys, or trucks in the case of smaller aircraft. The use of containers in wide-bodied aircraft has speeded up the process of baggage handling, as individual pieces no longer require to be handled on the apron. Instead they are loaded into aluminium containers which are profiled to the cross-section of the freight hold of the aircraft. Once loaded, these containers are rolled on to trucks or trailer trains which are driven out on to the apron where they are in turn loaded into the aircraft's hold by an elevating loader, identical to the freight loaders described in the next chapter; indeed, on wide-bodied transports the hold will be filled with a mixture of freight and baggage.

Smaller aircraft types are not able to use the facility of containerisation, owing to the limited size of their baggage holds. Instead, they continue to be loaded manually. Most modern medium-haul transports are low enough to the ground to enable baggage to be loaded direct from the apron; others, however, require the services of a conveyor loader to bridge the gap between the baggage trucks and the hatch.

The handling of incoming baggage is slightly less complicated than that of outgoing, although the process of getting it from the aircraft to the handling area is the exact reverse of that detailed above. Once in the handling area, though, it is a matter of waiting for the next available baggage carousel and loading all the bags from the flight, which is indicated at the passengers' end of the equipment, on to the associated belt which will carry them into the reclaim area.

Whilst in the handling area, both incoming and outgoing baggage is scrutinised by the security and customs authorities for contraband or explosives. HM Customs uses dogs trained to sniff out drugs in a locked suitcase. If any piece of luggage is judged to be suspect, a message will be relayed to colleagues in the reclaim area who will watch for those claiming the bag and detain them.

Boarding

Meanwhile, back in the departure lounge when the flight is called the passengers will make their way to the boarding gate, from whence they will board the aircraft. At many modern airports passengers are able to board directly via airbridges; at smaller, less busy airports the volume of traffic cannot justify the capital cost of such equipment so passengers enplane either from buses or by walking directly across the apron to the steps on to the aircraft. Although the latter would seem to be the ideal, there are drawbacks, particularly with the weather. It is also less than ideal from a safety point of view; a busy apron can be a dangerous place for those not used to it, so extra supervision is needed. Allied to this is the disruption to vehicular traffic caused by streams of passengers having to cross service roadways to reach their stand.

Most airports include stands which are some distance from the terminal complex. Buses are the only means usually used to gain access to these, although mobile lounges are used at some overseas locations. These are large passenger vehicles which are able to dock with both the terminal building and the aircraft,

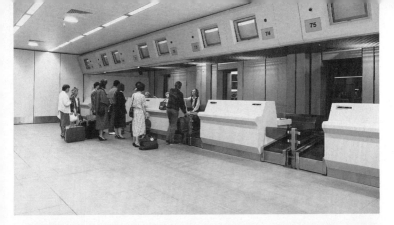

Top:
Check-in desks at Manchester Airport. The information display screens can be seen above, whilst the baggage conveyors can be seen exiting to the handling area.
Manchester Airport

Above:
Van Hool-bodied Scania coaches employed for shuttling between terminals and car parks at Heathrow. *Scania (Great Britain) Ltd*

Below:
Special electric truck used for returning baggage trolleys to terminals from the car parks at Heathrow. *Smiths Electric Vehicles*

Above:
Iveco-Ford 'Cargo' baggage vehicle carrying baggage into the handling area. The vehicle in the background appears to be a toilet service unit; also of interest are the built-in airstairs fitted into the tail of the Boeing 727. *Jonathan Falconer*

Below:
Catering vehicle built on Ford 'D' series chassis, seen here in travelling configuration. *Locomotors*

Above right:
A similar vehicle, this time using a Bedford 'TL' chassis, in its elevated position. Note the jacks which stabilise the chassis and the sturdy elevating mechanism. The bridge over the cab is telescopic to facilitate fine adjustment with the aircraft's door. *Edbro*

Right:
Catering vehicle mounted on a special low-profile chassis, with the cab dropped ahead of the front axle. This allows the front of the body to match more easily with lower door heights than with a conventional vehicle. *Author*

Below right:
Frantic activity around a Lufthansa Airbus A310-203. A catering truck is at the galley door, whilst containers are being handled at the entrance to the hold. The Bedford 'KM' in the middle distance is carrying two freight containers: the front one profiled to fit beside another in a lower hold, its neighbour designed to fill the full width of a main cabin. *Jonathan Falconer*

Above:
Two toilet service units, based on Iveco-Ford 'Cargo' chassis. *Jonathan Falconer*

Below:
Cabin cleaning vehicle and a fresh water tanker beneath the tail of a Norwegian SAS Douglas DC-9-81. *Jonathan Falconer*

Above:
A Danish SAS Douglas DC9 at Heathrow's Terminal 2. The telescopic airbridge is clearly visible in this view. *Author*

Below:
Electric baggage vehicle as used at Jersey Airport. *Smiths Electric Vehicles*

Above:
Baggage being loaded into the hold of an Airbus A310. On the left is a conveyor loader whilst on the right a container is being lifted by a loader. *Avialift*

Below:
Baggage being loaded by a conveyor into the rear hold of a British Airways Boeing 747-236B. *Avialift*

their height being adjustable to compensate for differing aircraft types.

The use of buses is more flexible and more cost effective than mobile lounges, as the buses used are frequently modifications of standard public service vehicles. The bodywork for such vehicles is often unusual in having entrance doors on both sides of the body; this saves much 'shunting' for the bus to line up with the foot of the steps. A design used at Heathrow involved the modification of a Leyland National bus to provide an entrance facing forward, beside the driver; the idea was for the bus to drive up to the steps, nose first. The passengers stepped straight off the bottom step into the bus.

Various designs of articulated bus have been tried with varying degrees of success. The most basic is a large, passenger-carrying semi-trailer, drawn by a standard commercial vehicle tractive unit. Many of these had a humped back appearance, as a deck was built over the coupling between tractor and trailer. These were somewhat basic, however, and the continental design of articulated bus (ie that with two parts joined by a flexible coupling in the middle) has been adopted at some UK airports, Luton being a good example. They have the advantage of good passenger-carrying capacity, but can be rather cumbersome on a busy apron.

Having arrived at the apron, the passenger has to climb the steps to board the aircraft. Many types of short and medium-haul transport incorporate power-operated steps which are part of the aircraft's structure, thereby dispensing with the use of movable steps at the airport. Although advantageous from an operational point of view, they suffer from the penalties of extra weight and complication.

The ground-based airstairs can be very involved pieces of equipment, needing to be very stable when extended up to the height of an aircraft door. The size and complexity varies from the lightweight steps which are towed behind a small tractor, to the large, adjustable steps mounted on a medium-weight lorry chassis which are required to serve a wide-bodied jet. These latter feature a staircase made in two sections, the upper section sliding over the lower to lengthen or shorten the entire unit, thereby accommodating different heights of aircraft. When the steps are extended, hydraulic jacks — mounted on outriggers — are lowered to increase the base area and the stability. In the medium-sized bracket, battery-electric chassis are popular for mounting steps on, as their mileages are low and the weight of their batteries is an aid to stability.

Facilities for disabled passengers

The assumption with all the procedures so far has been that the passenger is able-bodied; this is not an assumption made by airport operators, however, as they have a good record in providing facilities for those with impaired mobility. If the passenger requests it, he or she can be met by an airport or airline representative who will assist them all the way to their flight. This assistance can be anything from a helping hand with baggage to fully-fledged medical facilities. Many airports provide battery-electric golf buggies to convey disabled passengers around the terminal, taking them all the way to the departure lounge. If the airport is equipped with airbridges, there is little difficulty in using a conventional wheelchair to board a flight; where steps have to be negotiated, however, things are a little more involved.

It is common for an airport to provide some means of lifting wheelchairs and stretchers aboard aircraft; at its simplest it can be a cabin which is lifted from the apron on the tines of a fork-lift truck. More suitable is the provision of a purpose-built ambulance with an elevating body, similar to the trucks used by the catering companies. With vehicles of this type the passenger is often able to complete formalities at the airport's medical centre and be conveyed directly to the apron, where the ambulance can lift to the height of the aircraft's door. In more serious cases, such as medical emergency transfers, a conventional ambulance will be escorted airside to collect the patient, allowing the road journey to hospital to begin as quickly as possible.

VIP passengers

A final group of special passengers are VIPs, who regularly come and go through airports. Some large airports provide VIP lounges, where such travellers can wait or give interviews or press conferences, as the press and news agencies keep a watchful eye on arrivals and departures. VIPs such as the Royal Family and senior political figures will not use the public terminal at all, but will use a remote part of the airfield, and one which is easily made secure.

Anyone using an airport has a right to special treatment, as every passenger is very important to the airport operator and the airline. Without our patronage all airports would soon be in dire straits. There has been much effort expended over recent years to make the use of airports more enjoyable and less confusing, whilst operators have realised the importance of non-aviation activities in providing revenue to subsidise their airside business. Given that air travel is becoming ever more commonplace, airport authorities have a continuing challenge in meeting public tastes and requirements.

Below:
Scania/Plaxton airside coach, working at Heathrow airport. This vehicle, like many of its type, features doors fitted to both sides to save time when driving up to the foot of the airstairs. The panel above the front wheelarch displays the flight number by means of an LCD display. *Scania (Great Britain) Ltd*

3 Cargo Operations

One of the major areas of growth in recent years has been that of air cargo. At BAA airports, for instance, there has been an increase of 27.6% in the tonnage of air cargo handled in 1987 compared with 1977. But this increase in volume tells only half the story; the value of much air cargo is out of proportion to its weight. The worth of cargo passing through Heathrow (£21.3 billion in 1985) makes it Britain's busiest port, based on the value of cargo handled. The days of the odd sack of mail and a few parcels being put aboard a passenger aircraft are long gone. Airfreight is now a very competitive, highly organised operation, with many different services on offer.

Whilst airfreight can still be relatively expensive compared with surface transport, the use of modern, economical aircraft has reduced the margin to a level where air transport can compete effectively for many traffics. Modern industrial and commercial economics are such that the reduction in stockholding allowed by fast delivery times can compensate for higher freight charges. The lower incidence of damage to goods is another factor in the equation.

The growth in size of passenger aircraft has led to an increase in the amount of cargo being carried on such flights. Using BAA figures again, the percentage of freight carried by passenger flights has risen from 46.1 in 1977/78 to 81.1 in 1986/87, which is even more surprising given the vast increase in tonnage over the period. Freight of literally all shapes and sizes now goes by air, ranging from items of mail at one extreme to entire aircraft and boats at the other. Airfreight is now seen as an extension of the production line, linking it with the customer in a fast, cost-effective manner.

Parcels

The parcels sector has shown a very energetic growth over the past decade. Most airports are now active during the night handling small turboprops on parcels operations on both UK and European services. Such aircraft are able to operate at these times owing to their low noise levels, whilst the introduction of the BAe 146 QT (Quiet Trader) will have the effect of offering a much larger, longer-range transport capable of night operation.

Airports can handle parcels traffic readily, requiring little in the way of specialised ground equipment. Parcels may be sorted and consolidated at the airport, clearing Customs as they go, or, in the case of domestic flights, may arrive pre-sorted from an operator's depot ready to be loaded directly from the carrier's vehicle. The carriage of documents and computer tapes and disks accounts for a large part of air parcels traffic.

The incidence of this parcels traffic has been very welcome to both airport operator and airline alike. It has led to better utilisation of aircraft and ground facilities, taking place as it does in the small hours when equipment would otherwise be idle. Many passenger aircraft now have the facility of quickly removable seats to allow their use as freighters during the night in order to capitalise on this traffic.

Mail

Very similar to the operation of parcels services is the Royal Mail operation. Over 12% of Britain's domestic first class mail is carried by air, with a network of routes covering the country. Many of these routes converge on the East Midlands Airport near Derby where an interchange between air, road and rail transport takes place, owing to the airport's proximity to both the M1 motorway and the major rail centre at Derby. In addition to these radial routes other, direct, services operate, notably a nightly two-way service linking London and Edinburgh using passenger aircraft minus seats. After each flight the aircraft used is refitted with the seats left by its sister which has flown in the opposite direction.

Naturally, the majority of overseas mail is carried by air, as it has for many years. Much of it is carried on scheduled passenger flights, although dedicated mail services may be used for European destinations. An indication of the importance of air mail can be gathered from the fact that over 145,000 tonnes passed through UK airports in 1985, against 59,000 tonnes 10 years previously

Cargo

Much air cargo is, like mail, of a very valuable nature. The speed and security of air transport makes it well suited to the carriage of such goods as bullion, jewels and banknotes. Whilst airborne, such cargo is virtually immune from theft, but once on the apron extreme care is taken over security. High value cargo will often be loaded directly into a security vehicle for onward delivery. Alternatively, it may be transferred to either a secure area of the transit shed or stored in the strongroom of the security company, sometimes on the airport site. Even though elaborate measures are taken to guard such cargo, constant vigilance is necessary. The concentration of valuables at airports means that robbery is a constant risk.

A large proportion of airlines operate their own cargo divisions, especially now that passenger transports have such cargo capacity in their belly holds. A customer could, therefore, place his cargo with one of these airlines directly, or he could use an airfreight agent, also known as a freight forwarder. The function of a freight agent is to act as a middle man between the customer and the carrier. As such he will receive goods from the customer, often arranging transport to the airport. Once there he will arrange for documentation to be raised, including Customs clearance, and for the consignment to be packed ready for transit. The agent will then find the most suitable airline to fly it to its destination, and will usually arrange for delivery at the far end. As the agent does not own any aircraft of his own, he is in a good position to bargain effectively with airlines, and his wide ranging contacts will allow him to find space on a flight at short notice, if necessary. The customer may not know — or even care — which airline is carrying his goods, but by using an agent will be able to dispense with much of the worry that the complex paperwork can cause.

Most airports now have sophisticated transit sheds where goods are received from road vehicles, weighed and packaged. Whilst there, HM Customs will inspect the consignment, if necessary, and the documents will be raised. Each piece will be entered into a computer system, linking all the airlines, agents and the Customs service. The progress of the goods can be monitored at any part of its journey by interrogating this system, which is also used as part of the invoicing procedure.

The process works in reverse for import cargo, with the exception that the Customs authorities will be more active, using sniffer dogs and X-ray equipment in the effort to detect drugs and other contraband.

Many airports operate as transhipment centres, taking cargo from incoming flights, sorting it and forwarding it to ongoing services. An instance of this is when a long-haul flight arrives carrying freight for either a European or UK destination involving a further flight. Several airlines operate fleets of trunk lorries, connecting main airports by road where this is more efficient than short-haul air services. Whilst awaiting forward movement, these goods are held in 'bonded' storage — that is, held in an area approved by the Customs where duty need not be paid. In effect, although sited on UK soil, these areas are not part of Britain!

The majority of airfreight is either palletised or containerised nowadays. When cargo is carried in the cargo hold of a wide-bodied jet below the passenger deck, it is packed into profiled containers similar to those used for baggage. The use of containers results in the same benefits as with their use for baggage, ie less risk of damage and greater speed of handling. Some smaller aircraft types are not suitable for the use of containers, notably types used for short-haul services. For such aircraft, cargo is still loaded by hand (known as 'handballing'). Small aircraft can be loaded from ground level, but aircraft with a higher door

Above:
Shorts Belfast SC5 freighter is seen being made ready at Stansted. The rear cargo ramp can be seen clearly in this photograph. The airtug in the foreground is in the livery of Servisair, a well-known ground handling contractor. *Heavylift*

Below:
Heavylift's CL-44 Guppy is loaded. *Heavylift*

Above:
This rear view of the same aircraft, clearly shows its swing tail where a Hi-lo elevating loader is in position. *Heavylift*

Below:
Availift battery-electric loader. The driving position elevates with the load platform to allow the operator the best view at all times. *Availift*

Above:
Loader/transporter loading a Lockheed C-130 Hercules of the Portuguese Air Force.
Availift

Below:
Cargo pallets are loaded into a BAe146 Quiet Trader. *Availift*

Some of the cargoes routinely carried by Heavylift aircraft.
All photos Heavylift

Above:
A pollution control vessel . . .

Below:
. . . aircraft components (a Fokker F28 in this case) . . .

Above:
. . . commercial vehicles and spares for a famine relief agency . . .

Below:
. . . And, of course, a giraffe!

Above:
The Douglas DC5 Tugmaster: this diesel-powered tractor is typical of those used for
cargo and general-purpose duties. *Douglas*

Below:
This Leyland 'Freighter' chassis forms the basis for an air cargo vehicle. *Locomotors*

height are loaded either with a conveyor truck or, occasionally, with fork-lift trucks. Goods such as flowers from the Channel Islands are handled in this way, using transports such as the Shorts 330.

For heavier cargo, special airfreight pallets are employed. These are strong, light platforms to which goods are secured using nylon straps similar to very strong seatbelt webbing. This is tensioned by means of hand-operated ratchets. Loose, easily damaged packages can be secured with a cargo net which is thrown over the goods and secured to the pallet; the use of containers and pallets greatly reduces the risk of damage and speeds loading and unloading. Aircraft such as the all-freight version of the 747 are able to accept full-sized, 8ft-square containers, similar to the seagoing boxes one can see being transported by road, except that they are constructed of aluminium rather than steel to save unladen weight. They are loaded into the fuselage of the 747 by rolling them through the lifting nose section.

Freight usually arrives at the airport by road vehicle, which is unloaded into the transit shed where the goods are packaged. Parcels will be consolidated into batches for each destination, and will be containerised. These containers will be moved into a holding area when full to await the arrival of their flight. All movement around the transit shed and into the aircraft will be on powered roller tracks; these are let into the loading docks and the beds of airside freight vehicles in the same manner as they are fitted into aircraft floors. Roller tracks, which can be raised and lowered, allow the pallet to be moved or locked into position.

When the aircraft is on the stand ready to load, cargo will be called forward from the transit shed where loads for individual aircraft will have been assembled. The pallets and containers will be taken airside on either a trailer train, lorry or transporter. Once on the apron the freight will be rolled on to a self-propelled cargo loader which will already be positioned against the aircraft door. These loaders, although differing in detail, are all broadly similar. They comprise either a diesel or electric power unit which supplies hydraulic power for both travel and loading functions, a driving/operating position and an elevating platform. This may be split into two sections, one which

is lined up with the aircraft, and the other a rear platform which shuttles between ground level and the level of the front platform. Both platforms have powered rollers or rubber belts to roll pallets into the hold. From the door, the aircraft's on-board mechanised rollers will transfer the cargo along the fuselage to its stowage position where it will be secured during the flight.

Whilst most large passenger aircraft carry freight in their belly holds, along with baggage, this concept is taken a stage further with the use of 'Combi' aircraft. These aircraft have a portion of the main deck partitioned off for use in a cargo capacity with the aid of a movable bulkhead; this allows a variable mix of seating and freight capacity to take account of differing traffic patterns. Although such combis can be a boon to the airlines operating lightly trafficked routes, there is a potential problem for the airport operator; combi aircraft often require their cargo to be unloaded on what is ostensibly a passenger apron, with consequent risk of congestion.

The variety of cargo which now travels as airfreight is bewildering. The traditional air cargo has been one where speed is essential to maintain the product in a marketable condition, a classic example are fresh flowers which, being both light and fairly valuable, are ideal for air cargo. Whilst such traffics are still well represented, they have been joined by a wide array of other goods. A traffic well suited to air freighting is electronic equipment; as with flowers, this equipment is relatively light, easily damaged and valuable — factors which make carriage by air economically desirable. More surprising items are commonplace: luxury cars, for example, are regularly delivered by air to save damage and ensure swift forwarding.

Whilst on the subject of cars, motor racing teams are virtually obliged to ship their entire operation by air when the grand prix circus leaves Europe for America or the Southern Hemisphere. Cars, spares, tools and everything are flown out, mainly because of the time factor. For the same reason racehorses are seasoned air travellers, with Stansted Airport handling many thoroughbreds because of its proximity to Newmarket, the centre of the British bloodstock community.

Livestock

Racehorses are not the only animals to be freighted by air. Animals of all shapes and sizes routinely make up air cargo, ranging from domestic pets to dolphins, and including valuable farm animals being exported for breeding along with exotic zoo animals being transferred between zoos as part of international breeding programmes. Most airports have a livestock centre as part of their facilities, the most famous being the one at Heathrow. Here, animals of all descriptions receive expert attention whilst they await collection. Many go straight from such a centre to a quarantine establishment until they have a clean bill of health to enter the UK.

Special Cargo

Temperature-controlled transport is another sector of airfreight that might surprise, perhaps. Fresh meat, vegetables and fruit are commonplace. This traffic is quickly transferred from airside to coldrooms which form part of the transit shed to await customs clearance and road transport to its final destination, or to await onward airfreight. Hazardous cargo is also handled by airports, subject to extremely rigorous safety conditions.

The obvious, oft quoted advantage of air cargo is speed. This advantage leads to the medium carrying many urgent spare parts. These spares can be anything from car or machine tool spares to very large pieces for ships or oil installations,

for instance. To handle such large 'lump' loads, airports tend to hire-in loading equipment such as mobile cranes. The load is lifted from road transport on to an elevating platform, from where it is rolled or winched into the cargo hold.

At the very top end of the weight carrying range are a handful of heavy air cargo specialists, the leader of these being HeavyLift, operating out of Stansted Airport in Essex. HeavyLift was far-sighted enough to acquire the ex-RAF Short Belfast freighters, having a payload of 36,500kg (80,500lb). Also operated is a 'Guppy' version of the Canadair CL-44, itself a licence-built verion of the Bristol Britannia. This aircraft has an outsized fuselage which is loaded via a swing tail. These aircraft are kept busy carrying a variety of cargo. An area in which HeavyLift specialises is the support of the international aerospace industry. This support includes the delivery of new helicopters inside the freighters, returning damaged aircraft to their manufacturers for repair, and moving aircraft components from sub-contractors for final assembly. Other cargo handled includes animals, boats, lorries and armoured vehicles.

Strangely enough, aircraft of the type used for heavy freight require very little in the way of ground support facilities. Being developments of military types these aircraft can operate from rudimentary airfields if required, so they can be largely self-sufficient. HeavyLift's Belfasts load over their own rear ramp which has a lifting capacity of 22,700kg (50,000lb) and can be used as a bridge between a lorry bed and the freight hold. The use of on-board loading equipment is indeed justified, made necessary by the low utilisation that ground-based machinery of that capacity would achieve.

Conventional cargo handling equipment, as touched upon earlier, comprises a range of lifting and transporting machines including fork-lift trucks, conveyors and elevating loaders. Besides general warehouse duties, fork-lifts can be used for lifting freight up to aircraft door height, but are not used much for intensive operations, this being the role of more specialised units such as the elevating loaders described above. Their use allows for quicker loading and unloading and efficient use of manpower. As the operation is split into two stages, one pallet can be loaded from a road vehicle whilst a second pallet is being handled into the aircraft from the top level.

Conveyor trucks are used for handling loose cargo and are basically light goods-type chassis mounting a hydraulic conveyor which can be adjusted easily to suit differing operating heights. The actual belt is often fitted with a photo-electric device to stop packages being pitched off the end of the conveyor if no one is at hand to take them. The prime mover is usually diesel, although battery-electric versions are used. Although most operators use separate lifting machines and trucks, one unit is available which combines both functions. This machine, known as a loader/transporter is capable of loading itself with pallets of cargo in the transit shed, transporting them airside and elevating them in the same way as an elevating platform. This versatility is potentially very useful where only odd pallets of cargo need to be loaded or unloaded on a passenger apron, cutting down as it does the number of vehicles present around the aircraft. To counter this is the effect of using an expensive piece of machinery for the transport function which could be undertaken by cheaper, less specialised trucks. But this is yet another balance to be struck by the airside operations department.

Above left:
Cargo containers being unloaded from the aft hold of a Lufthansa Airbus A310-203. A container is emerging from the hold on to a loader; an electric tractor waits with a string of trolleys. *Jonathan Falconer*

Below:
The Scania 112M with drawbar trailer is used by British Airways for overland trunking of cargo between UK airports. *Scania (Great Britain) Ltd*

4 Apron Technical Services

Whilst an aircraft is being turned around its health is being checked and maintained by a small army of ground technicians who will be working feverishly to complete the huge task in the brief time allotted.

Power supplies

Before any work can be done, arrangements for electrical power for the aircraft will be made for such services as lighting, radios and avionics and power for the cleaning staff. In flight electric and hydraulic power is generated by the main engines, so when these are shut down an alternative source has to be found. Large airliners generate and use electricity at 115/200V alternating current (ac), with a frequency of 400 cycles/sec (Hz). Smaller aircraft work with 28V direct current (dc). In Britain the mains supplies electricity at 240V ac at a frequency of 50Hz, so one cannot simply plug an extension cable into a 13amp socket!

Many modern airliners have an auxiliary power unit (APU) in the tail. In essence this is a gas turbine power unit providing electrical power at the correct standard along with hydraulic power and air bled from the compressor stage for air conditioning and engine starting. This APU is usually started during the approach phase to be ready to take the load when the main engines spool down. In addition the APU has an emergency function should there be a fault in the aircraft's main power system. On a short turn around this means it is used for ground power until main engine start, but other means are usually found for anything but the shortest stop. Many airports are unwilling to allow APU running for any longer than necessary because of pollution from the turbine exhaust and the shrill noise. APU running is minimised by the aircraft operator to save fuel, as this is drawn from the main supply tanks; as the APU is maintained on a timed basis, any excessive use will also result in increased maintenance.

The way round the problem is to supply electrical power from outside the aircraft whilst on the apron, at the correct voltage and frequency. This power reaches the aircraft via a flexible cable plugged into a receptacle in the belly near the nose undercarriage door, having been generated by either a ground power unit (GPU) or a 400Hz distribution system.

The GPU is basically a powerful diesel engine driving an alternator, the whole unit being mounted either on a trailer, on an airtug or being self-propelled. The unit has of course to be far more sophisticated than that in order to fulfil the very precise requirements of a modern avionics system. The diesel power unit is usually a derivative of an automotive (commercial vehicle) engine, but with ultra-sensitive governing to maintain its speed, and therefore the frequency of the electrical output within very tight limits. Many different types of diesel engine are used, notably Perkins, Cummins or the air-cooled Deutz engine.

As already stated, smaller aircraft utilise a 28V dc power system. To feed this, most GPUs have a dc output, or if there is sufficient need a smaller dc only GPU may be provided. When trailer-mounted, the GPU suffers from having need of a tractor of some sort to move it from task to task, which inevitably means an extra machine to clutter the apron. When an aircraft is enjoying a long stopover, for instance a freighter loading a lump cargo, this may not be a disadvantage. On a busy passenger ramp, however, congestion may be so acute that the GPU will be airtug-mounted or self-propelled.

When mounted on a tug, the GPU occupies no apron space other than that of its host vehicle. It does, however, commit a very expensive machine (ie the tug) for the whole time that electric power is required, not an ideal situation from the point of view of utilisation. A partial solution is to make the GPU self-propelled, either by mounting the whole assembly on a truck chassis or by using the main engine to power the road wheels; an example is the Houchin Model 701 which uses a Deutz 182bhp V8 diesel to both power the alternator and provide automotive power. This allows the unit to move itself and also to undertake light towing duties; useful, for instance, in towing the crew steps out of the way to clear the apron prior to main engine start at the end of the turn around.

What appears to be a Volkswagen Transporter van with a vacuum cleaner hose on the front bumper may sometimes be seen in attendance on the apron. This is in fact the Garrett Jet Air Starter, built in West Germany by Garrett GmbH. Inside the van is what amounts to an aircraft GPU which, although usually used for engine starting, is capable of providing ground power and air-conditioning air, all in a very compact package.

Mobile GPUs, as described above, all suffer from two major drawbacks: they take up space and cause pollution. As we have seen, space around an aircraft during turn around is at a premium, and the congestion arising from the many vehicles causes an added hazard in an already hazardous environment, risking injury to staff and perhaps passengers along with damage to both aircraft and vehicles. The pollution is caused by fumes and noise, and the possibility of fuel and oil being dripped on to the apron.

Many airports are now using a 400Hz ground distribution system which overcomes all the disadvantages of mobile equipment. The system employs a stationary frequency converter, basically a 50Hz motor driving a 400Hz alternator which supplies high voltage electrical power via switchgear and circuit breakers to transformers sited on each stand. These step the voltage down to the required 115/200V. The power reaches the aircraft by means of a flexible cable which either trails across the apron, is supported by an articulated framework, or is festooned along the outside of a telescopic airbridge.

As mains electricity is used as the prime mover, the system is quiet and clean and has relatively low operating costs. It does have drawbacks in its high initial cost and its lack of flexibility, although cost can be recovered by virtue of its economy of operation. The lack of flexibility is of no consequence at modern passenger terminals, however, as aircraft always occupy specific stands. For outlying stands not coupled to the distribution system mobile GPU equipment continues to be used.

Refuelling

A universal requirement of any aircraft is that of fuel, and fuel of the correct grade and quality must be supplied at the right time and in the right quantity. Aviation fuel is divided into two broad types:

● *Aviation Gasoline (AVGAS)* — this is based on petrol (gasoline) and is used for piston-engined aircraft. Owing to its low flashpoint it is highly flammable and is treated with the greatest care. There are, in turn, three grades of AVGAS — AVGAS 80, 100 and 100LL, dyed red, green and blue respectively to help prevent accidental misdelivery. This must be avoided as aircraft piston engines are designed to run on one grade of fuel only.

● *Aviation Turbine Fuel (AVTUR)* — this is based on paraffin oil (kerosene) and is burned in the turbine engines of jet and turboprop transports. Again there are different types — Jet A and Jet A1. These are much safer than AVGAS, having a higher flashpoint. Jet A1 is the most widely used by civil aviation.

Whatever type of fuel is supplied, purity is an absolute priority. Small quantities of dirt or water in fuel could cause wear, corrosion or even a 'flame out' — a total loss of power owing to loss of combustion in a turbine engine. Every care is taken to prevent any contaminant being delivered to the aircraft, as we will see.

Fuel is delivered to the airport's tank farm either by road, rail or pipeline. The demands for jet fuel at a major airport usually preclude the use of road transport. Heathrow, for instance, receives its fuel from pipelines fed from several sources, so no surface transport is involved from the refinery.

Before being pumped into the storage tanks, usually inside the security fence, the fuel passes through water separators and filters. When it has settled, the fuel is checked for the presence of water and dirt, both by checking that a sample is clear and bright and by chemical tests. From the tank farm the fuel reaches the aircraft in one of two ways: either by hydrant or tanker. In the case of AVGAS, delivery is always by tanker, because nowadays quantities are fairly small. Jet A1 however could be delivered by either means, depending on the airport.

Some years ago, particularly when wide-bodied transports were introduced, it was realised that to refuel such large aircraft with tankers would involve either very large vehicles or too many smaller ones, leading in both cases to unacceptable congestion on the apron. When a 747 is capable of uplifting around 150 tons of fuel, the scale of the problem can be visualised. The remedy was to install hydrant refuelling systems — networks of pipes leading from the tank farm and buried under the apron.

From the storage tanks the fuel passes through another set of filters and water separators to pumps which are switched in and out of circuit automatically; this is in order to maintain the required pressure in the pipes according to the amount being drawn off at that moment. From there it passes under the runways and taxiways to hydrants, sited in pits covered by steel plates on the apron. These hydrants are fitted with valves and connectors to which the fuel dispensers connect. These dispensers are the small, complicated-looking vehicles seen in the liveries of the major oil companies. They are not normally equipped with a pump, as the pressure generated by the pumps at the tank farm is sufficient to force the fuel into the aircraft tanks. The plumbing aboard the dispenser is indeed very complex, but the main components are:

● *Inlet Hose* — fitted with wheels to ease the task of dragging it over the ground. The coupling which mates with the hydrant in the pit incorporates a pressure control valve and a 'dead man' valve to shut the fuel flow down in the event of an emergency
● *Filters and separators for water and air*
● *Surge Suppressor* — this is a large vessel which damps out any violent fluctuations in hydrant pressure which could damage either the dispenser or aircraft
● *Meter* — used to ensure that the fuel amount ordered by the flight crew is actually delivered, and that the airline is correctly invoiced
● *Delivery Valves* — used to contol the flow of fuel into the aircraft

● *Delivery Hoses* — sometimes up to four are fitted, two in the elevating platform (qv) for fillers in aircraft wings, and two on power-operated reels for low-mounted fillers
● *Elevating Platform* — allowing access to high-level fuel fillers
● *Dump Tank* — after delivery the hoses remain pressurised and, consequently, fairly rigid. To make them easier to handle the pressure is released into the dump tank, which is periodically emptied back into the delivery circuit.

When delivering, the first operation is to connect, or bond, the dispenser to both the hydrant and the aircraft by means of a cable. This ensures that all the elements of the system have the same electrical charge, reducing the risk of static electricity causing sparks. The hoses are then connected up, but before delivery a sample of fuel is taken to prove its purity. The inlet and delivery valves are opened and the required amount of fuel delivered. When delivery is complete, the pressure is released from the hoses into the dump tank, and the hoses rewound. The inlet hose is uncoupled and only then is the electrical bonding disconnected. The meter readings are agreed and the dispenser is then free to repeat the process on another stand.

Whilst a hydrant system is universal at airports such as Heathrow and Gatwick, it does suffer from some drawbacks. Being a fixed system it lacks flexibility, and there is also a very high capital cost to installing the underground pipes, pumps etc, along with the considerable disruption connected with the installation work. For this reason work is often incorporated into a major airport redevelopment project.

Such systems are normally owned and operated by a consortium of oil companies. Each company accounts for the fuel drawn in its name by means of the meters on the dispensers. An indication of the capabilities of a modern system can be gained by looking at Heathrow where the main system serves about 50 stands and is capable of delivering 22,000gal/min, whilst a separate system with a capacity of 3,000gal/min serves the freight area.

Where traffic density cannot warrant the capital cost of hydrants, and for outlying stands at major airports, fuel tankers continue to be used. These appear similar to tankers used for delivering to

Above:
Turnround: fuel being pumped aboard whilst the cable in the foreground supplies 400Hz electric power. *BP Oil Ltd*

Below:
Diesel GPU, showing connection to the aircraft's power system. *Author*

Above:
An Air France Boeing 737-228 being serviced. A fuel dispenser mounted on a Ford Transit chassis is delivering via connections in the wings. At the same time, baggage is unloaded from the forward hold by means of a conveyor loader. *Jonathan Falconer*

Below:
A Ford 'D' series-based dispenser provides fuel for a Boeing 747. The elevating platform and rear hose reel are prominent in this view. *BP Oil Ltd*

Above:
This articulated refueller is drawn by a Seddon-Atkinson tractive unit. Although based on road-going vehicles, units such as this are uprated to operate at much greater weights. *BP Oil Ltd*

Below:
Fuel hoses are connected to the underwing fuelling points of a 747. *BP Oil Ltd*

Above:
Low-profile tankers are designed to operate beneath aircraft wings. The platform at the rear elevates, carrying the hoses with it. *BP Oil Ltd*

Below:
Fuel being supplied to a Sikorsky S61N helicopter. *BP Oil Ltd*

Above:
Refuelling in progress, with the operative checking an underwing dipstick. Note the electrical bonding wire connected to the nosewheel assembly. *BP Oil Ltd*

Below:
Vestergaard de-icer unit on Scania chassis. The vehicle is used for spraying de-icing fluid on to wings and upper fuselage areas. *Scania (Great Britain) Ltd*

Left:
The Douglas ET3 Tugmaster, an electric airtug, is seen demonstrating its four-wheel steering. *Douglas*

Below left:
The Douglas DC12 Tugmaster, a heavy diesel machine weighing more than 45 tonnes, shows its dual, elevating cabs. *Douglas*

Bottom left:
This County/Hallam airtug is fitted with a heavy-duty hydraulic winch for aircraft recovery work. *Country Tractors*

Below:
Pushback commences for an SAS Douglas DC9. In the background can be seen a heavy airstairs unit on a Dodge chassis. *Jonathan Falconer*

Bottom:
As the aircraft swings into position for departure, the ground engineer is seen walking alongside the nose, talking to the flightcrew via a headset and wander lead.
Jonathan Falconer

Above:
The ground engineer holds the jackplug of his communications lead aloft, thus proving to the flightcrew that he is no longer connected. *Jonathan Falconer*

Below:
The DC9 makes its way along the apron centreline towards the taxiway.
Jonathan Falconer

filling stations, but beneath the skin there are important differences. Firstly — and once again — refuelling tankers carry extensive filtration and separation equipment. They are also fitted with power-operated hose reels in the same way as a dispenser. Unlike dispensers, however, tankers are fitted with a powerful pump driven by a power take-off from the main engine. Equipment is frequently included to allow such vehicles to de-fuel aircraft on the odd occasions when this is necessary, for instance when fuel tanks need emptying prior to an aircraft going for major maintenance. The tanker pumps the contents of the aircraft's tanks into its own, which in turn is then emptied into separate storage from where it is ultimately returned to the airline from whence it came.

As the airport roads are not governed by Department of Transport rules and regulations as are public highways, vehicles confined to them need not be restricted to the regulations governing weights and dimensions. As a result, although refuellers are based on road-going lorry chassis, they are usually uprated to far above the weights allowed on public highways. A popular configuration for airport tankers is a four-wheeled rigid vehicle towing a four-wheeled drawbar trailer. The tank of this is connected to the pump of the drawing vehicle by a hose which can be seen supported over the drawbar. Such an outfit has better turning geometry than an articulated tanker, so is less likely to suffer accidental damage — or cause it. Many articulated tankers are to be seen, however, some of which betray their carrying capacity by their immense size.

Minor maintenance

Whilst all the foregoing is happening, many other tasks need attention. Small tankers may be seen, for instance, topping up lubricating oil on piston-engined aircraft (turbine engines use very little oil, so are topped up only during inspections), whilst oxygen supplies are replenished from cylinders mounted on a trolley.

Minor faults which develop during the inbound flight will be radioed ahead on the company frequency, and engineers will be waiting to clear any notified defects, providing these are of a minor nature. Such minor faults could include navigation lamps being defective, or one of the cockpit instruments giving a suspect reading. The service engineers may be employed by the airline owning the aircraft or, if it is away from base, either an aviation engineering company or another airline having a maintenance agreement with the operator. This explains why engineers from one airline can be seen working on another's aircraft.

Service vehicles used by the ground maintenance staff are often ordinary vans although, as ever, the Land Rover is very popular. Some mechanical means by which control surfaces and engines can be reached is often fitted, either in the form of a simple platform on the bonnet and roof of a Land Rover perhaps, or in some cases a hydraulically-operated access cage.

Now and again it will be necessary to change a wheel and tyre on an aircraft during turn around. This is accomplished by using a special trailer which carries the fresh wheels and tyres in a low-slung pannier arrangement, along with a heavy-duty hydraulic jack and the tools needed for the job. Bottles of nitrogen are carried, both to power the wrenches and to inflate the tyres to their correct pressure once fitted. Nitrogen is used in aircraft tyres to reduce the risk of explosion following such an incident as a brake fire, because it is an inert gas.

Special precautions are needed during freezing conditions. Before take-off all aircraft must be free of ice and snow on their wings, control surfaces and fuselage. Besides the obvious risk of control surfaces freezing solid and the added weight, there is also a great risk of an aircraft's aerodynamics being spoiled by ice, with consequent loss of lift. This problem is combated by the application of an antifreeze solution before taxying out. The techniques used differ: in Scandinavia, where the problem is greater than in the UK, some installations use a huge arch through which the aircraft is towed rather like a giant car-wash spray.

In the UK this level of sophistication could not be justified, and the process is carried out using hydraulic platforms mounted on commercial chassis, ranging from 35cwt Transit-type vehicles through to large, specialised units which may heat the solution before spraying. The latest machines used by British Airways, as an

Above:
A County/Hallam airtug is seen here handling a Boeing 727. *County Tractors*

example, were specially designed in Denmark by Vestergaard and incorporate an enclosed platform allowing greater comfort and safety for the operators. At other times of the year, and at many airports, such vehicles are used for general duties which require elevated access.

Engine starting

As already stated, most large modern airliners are fitted with an auxiliary power unit (APU). This is generally started up even when it has not been used to provide ground power, in order to provide power for main engine starting.

Nearly all large turbojet and turbofan engines are started by compressed air driving a high-speed turbine, clutched into the accessory gearbox of the engine. This is largely to save the weight of an electric starter motor of the same power, and also because of the availability of bleed air from engines already running to start a dead engine.

Some older aircraft, however, do not carry an APU so a source of compressed air must be found on the ground. This source is usually an Air Start Unit (ASU), which has the appearance of a large GPU, either trailer or truck-mounted. The vitals of the ASU comprise a very powerful diesel engine driving a screw-type compressor which delivers air, via a filter, to a large-diameter hose to the pneumatic system of the aircraft. Because the starter on the engne is a turbine, it requires huge quantities of medium-pressure air to power it. Although the operating pressure is only 42lb/sq in, the volume demanded dictates the use of a very powerful power unit. The ASU will normally appear just before departure time, although it can be used as a source of air-conditioning air, in which case it will be in use for a longer time. A special air-conditioning unit will be used more often, however.

Starting air may be provided from the ground in two other ways: a jet air starter, as mentioned in the section about electric power, is basically an aircraft APU mounted in a van or on a trailer. It operates by providing bleed air in exactly the same way as it would in an aircraft. The second option is engaging in its simplicity: it is merely a large compressed air tank on wheels. This is charged up from a static compressor, or from a workshop air system, and is then towed to the apron where air is supplied to the aircraft via a pressure reduction valve which reduces the high pressure in the vessel to the moderate pressure required by the aircraft. The disadvantage of this system is that the air reservoir needs recharging after a small number of starts, but, for an airport with only an occasional need for ground starting, this may not be a huge problem.

If a large aircraft starts from a ground source it is usual to start only one engine — ie the one supplying hydraulic power for brakes and steering — from the starter unit. This is to save the tug having to push back against the thrust of the engines, even at ground idle settings. When an internal APU is used, the first engine is started as the aircraft is being pushed back.

In the case of smaller aircraft such as turboprops, electric starting is employed. The power for this comes from either internal batteries or, more often, from the GPU which, in the case of a 28V dc unit, has the facility to run at a higher speed than normal for short periods in order to generate the power required for starting.

Pushback

Most modern airports now operate nose-in stands as discussed earlier. One obvious result of this is that some means has to be found to push the aircraft out on to the taxiway, as the sight of aircraft rocketing backwards is strictly reserved for Lockheed Hercules at air displays! The operation is known, logically enough, as 'pushback' or 'pushout'.

The vehicles used to provide motive power for pushback range from small tractors closely akin to agricultural tractors, to airtugs looking as though they had come straight out of the pages of science fiction. Small aircraft like the Shorts 330/360 are frequently handled by lighter, less powerful tractors of the type used for handling baggage etc. When moving up to aircraft of greater weight and size, however, more power and manoeuvrability is called for. These needs are met by a range of very sophisticated pushback tractors, or airtugs, as they are commonly called. Although used primarily for pushing back, such airtugs are also used for towing dead aircraft around the airport — to and from parking areas, for instance.

Power, traction and manoeuvrability are the keynotes for airtugs. Power is again provided by automotive-type diesel engines: Perkins, Deutz and Cummins are popular choices, many operators choosing the same make of engine for a whole range of machinery to simplify spares and maintenance. The larger examples of these machines use a torque converter transmission, delivering power to all four wheels. The use of a torque converter provides for a very smooth start, whilst the elimination of a friction clutch reduces maintenance costs significantly. Many airtugs are fitted with four-wheel steering as well as four-wheel drive. This makes these machines very nimble for their size, the most sophisticated examples having the choice of two-wheel steering, four-wheel opposed steering (where the front and rear axles steer on opposite locks) and crab steering (where the axles steer on the same lock allowing the tractor to move diagonally). This last mode is particularly useful for aligning the tug to the nosewheel of the aircraft.

The largest units are built to a very low overall height, because the distance from the nose tip to the nosewheel of a 747 is

Fig 16 Airtug steering modes

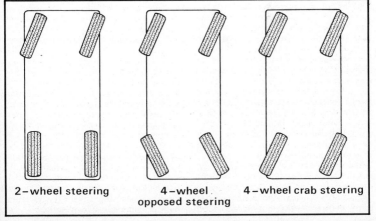

2–wheel steering   4–wheel opposed steering   4–wheel crab steering

so great that the tug must actually work under the fuselage. Thus one of the largest units, the Douglas Tugmaster DC-14, which weighs around 70 tons and has a 384bhp (286kW) Deutz engine, has an overall height of no more than 5ft 3in (1,600mm). Because of the limited view from a cab of this height a hydraulic lift can be fitted which raises the cab by 2ft (610mm) to provide a better view when travelling around the airport, thereby increasing safety. A further refinement often seen is the fitting of a second cab at the rear of the vehicle, housing a second driver to drive back out of the path of the departing aircraft, as the rear view from the front cab is inadequate for operating in such a hazardous environment.

Tugs serving smaller aircraft need not be built to such extreme height limitations as their big sisters, the aircraft nosewheel being much nearer to the nose tip. Many of the features of the larger machines are still to be found, such as four-wheel drive and torque converter transmission, but the greater height of the driving position makes the elaborate second cab un-necessary. These smaller units are, once again, much heavier than they look — typically about 25 tons. This is achieved by such measures as fitting cast iron mud-wings as ballast.

There is currently much interest in the use of electric airtugs for several reasons, primarily that of cost. Compared with diesel tractors, electric tractors are significantly more expensive to purchase owing to the cost of their batteries. Their lower running and maintenance costs, however, mean that the 'whole life' cost of the vehicle is lower. The introduction of thyristor control circuits, which can control electric power without waste, have improved the economics of the situation. Electric vehicles are quiet and clean, although to the layman that would seem insignificant in an airside environment! Such tugs do need to be recharged, of course, but the period between full charges can be extended by the use of 'opportunity charging' — that is, putting the unit on charge during quiet periods of the day to top the batteries up. All this, however, would need very careful management to ensure that enough fully-charged tugs are available at the right time.

Finally a word about the actual towbar: it, like almost everything else at an airport, is not as it seems. Towbars are designed exclusively for one type of aircraft, which explains why there are often a number of them parked together on a corner of the apron waiting for use. The actual bar — or rather, tube — needs to be manufactured and tested to the highest standard to equip it for the rigours of many years of pushing and pulling 747s. Many towbars also have a manual hydraulic jack to raise the coupling to the height of the nosewheel assembly, and to retract the roadwheels. Some smaller types dispense with the hydraulics as the bar is light enough to manhandle.

5 Aircraft Maintenance

Most airports feature hangars on their perimeters in which repairs and maintenance are carried out on aircraft using the field. The word 'hangar', like many words in aviation parlance, comes from a French word meaning a horse-shoeing shed; how times change! Inside these hangars engineers perform the involved tasks required to maintain a modern transport aircraft in an airworthy condition.

Legislation

The term 'airworthy condition' implies a condition that is not negotiable. Minimum conditions are laid down by the aircraft manufacturers in conjunction with bodies such as the CAA in the UK or Federal Aviation Administration (FAA) in the USA. To ensure uniformity, these conditions are incorporated into the Joint Airworthiness Requirements, which are international conditions applied by each country's civil aviation body.

In the UK it is the CAA's responsibility to monitor and control all aspects of airworthiness. It will be involved from a very early stage in the design of a new aircraft type; CAA engineers will vet the plans for it and be involved in prototype manufacture and testing. The aircraft will only be granted the vital Certificate of Airworthiness (C of A) after a very comprehensive programme of testing, during which time the maintenance aspects of the design will also have been under scrutiny. Following certification, any modifications to the airframe or powerplant will need to be re-certified in a similar way.

The question of repairs and servicing will be uppermost in the minds of the manufacturers from the very beginning of the design process; all aircraft builders strive to build commercial transports which will be as economical to maintain as possible. Maintenance costs amount to a major component in the 'whole life' cost of operating a particular aircraft type, not only in terms of the cost of spares and engineering man-hours, but in the loss of availability. With present-day jet transports costing millions of pounds each, every minute not earning revenue is critical.

Inspection

Against these requirements, however, must be set the overriding concern for safety. Modern aircraft are constructed with massive reserves of strength to help ensure this safety, whilst systems are duplicated or triplicated to guard against a failure. The CAA, or its equivalent, must be absolutely certain of an aircraft type's integrity before it is certified, and detailed maintenance schedules and procedures will be inspected and approved as part of the certification process.

The CAA's involvement with the engineering aspect of air safety is all-encompassing; before a licence can be granted to an operator he must satisfy the CAA that proper arrangements have been made for inspection and servicing of his fleet. Many large operators carry out their own maintenance at their home bases, but such is the capital outlay required for the necessary buildings and equipment that this is an avenue closed to a small airline. Because of the cost of the facilities mentioned above, most large operators undertake 'third party' work, that is work on aircraft other than their own. This work may, indeed, be on the aircraft of an airline in competition with the host. By undertaking third party work, maintenance staff and equipment can be utilised to maximum advantage, thereby spreading its cost over a broader base. By the same token, the smaller airline benefits by having access to the specialised facilities required by the CAA. Airlines tend to get a reputation for work on the type of aircraft which make up their own fleet, and the expertise built up by their staff can help in their securing third party work on that particular make or type. Even if an operator owns his own engineering establishment he will, in turn, be in the hands of others when away from base. If a fault develops during an outward flight he will have to seek assistance from either another operator, with whom he probably has an agreement for such an eventuality, or a specialist aviation engineering company.

These companies exist only to provide engineering support to operators, not owning any aircraft of their own. Many of the larger airlines have, however, now constituted their engineering divisions as separate companies making them, in fact, aviation engineering contractors in their own right. The logic behind this is to create autonomous operations that can pursue third party work more actively, whilst providing a separate profit centre within the airline.

The engineers who work on aircraft are all personally licensed by the CAA, and are not permitted to work in an area of expertise outside their own. When working on an aircraft, therefore, technicians will operate as a team, each contributing their own particular skill.

Servicing and maintenance

The emphasis on aviation preventative maintenance has shifted over recent years; the time-honoured method relied on 'lifing' critical components, meaning that each was given a life expressed in terms of flying hours or elapsed time for airframe and engines, or landings in the case of undercarriage units. After this lifetime was exceeded, the part was replaced by either a new or reconditioned unit, irrespective of the condition of the original. Although this system ensured that aircraft were always in an 'as new' condition, it was realised that there was much waste in terms of both materials and labour. So whilst it remains the norm for older aircraft, a new system known as condition monitoring has been developed, with the close involvement of the aviation authorities, to apply to newer civil types.

Condition monitoring relies on the continual assessment of the actual condition of the aircraft and its components and systems. So, whilst there are major savings to be made in the areas of components and man-hours, ultra-sophisticated inspection techniques are required to ensure that all vital areas are thoroughly sound. The monitoring process incorporates a statistical element, examining the service history of both individual aircraft and entire types to highlight any trends which may lead to problems. These trends may then lead to modifications to the relevant maintenance schedules. This concept is taken a stage further with the fitting of data recorders (separate from the famous 'black boxes') which record such information as engine pressures and temperatures. The data recorded is analysed by computers at the airline's engineering base, and any abnormality automatically noticed by the interpretive equipment; this in turn alerts engineers to, perhaps, an incipient malfunction.

During scheduled maintenance which is carried out at predetermined intervals, much use is made of the very latest technology for the task of examining the aircraft. In the case of power units, for instance, a mass of information can be gathered by analysing the used lubricating oil after it is drained. This oil is examined by means of a spectrograph which indicates minute traces of metals in suspension. The results will show, by means of the concentration and type of metal found, if abnormal wear is taking place, and whereabouts in the engine it is occurring. Further evidence is provided by the fitting of magnetic plugs in the lubrication system which collect any ferrous particles.

Instruments known as borescopes have been adapted from surgical instruments for the examination of the interior of turbine engines without extensive stripping. These fibre optic devices are inserted through specially provided inspection ports to allow such components as turbine and compressor blades to be looked at.

The airframe itself is inspected using a number of techniques: both X-ray and gamma ray equipment is employed for detecting cracks in wing spars, fuselage frames and so on. The method is fundamentally similar to that used in hospital: a weak source of radiation is placed on one surface of the component under scrutiny and a special photographic plate on the other. The result will show a fracture in exactly the same way as it would for a broken leg. Ultrasound is also used for the same purpose: high frequency sound waves are projected into

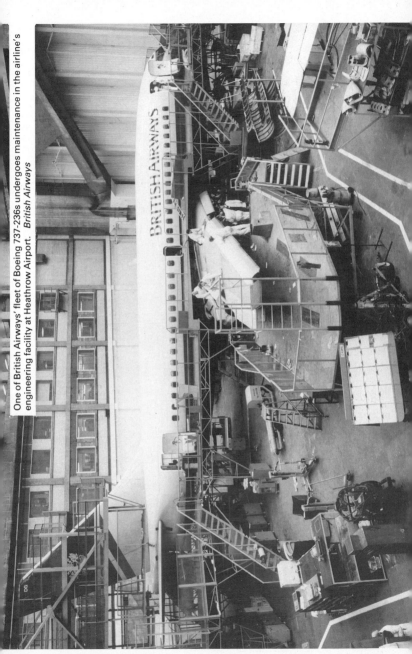

One of British Airways' fleet of Boeing 737-236s undergoes maintenance in the airline's engineering facility at Heathrow Airport. *British Airways*

Above:
Work is carried out on one of British Airways' seven Concordes at the airline's
Cranebank maintenance facility. *British Airways*

Above:
Technicians work on the Olympus powerplants of a British Airways Concorde.
British Airways

Left:
A turbofan power unit being serviced. *British Airways*

Above:
Tail dock surrounding the tail of an Air 2000 Boeing 757-28A at the Luton facility of Monarch Aircraft Engineering. *Author*

Below:
A British Airways Boeing 757 and an Airways-Cymru BAC One-Eleven are photographed surrounded by staging. *Author*

Above:
Engineers attend to the Rolls-Royce RB211 engines of the Boeing 757. *Author*

Below and below right:
Turbofan engines are tended in the powerplant shop. Note the covers over the intakes to prevent damage to the blading. *Author*

Fig 17 Maintenance schedule as applied by Monarch Aircraft Engineering to Boeing 757 aircraft

'A' check Before each cycle (flight); walk-round looking for leaks, damage etc, carried out by ground engineer at base, first officer if away from base.

'B' check Daily, as 'A' but more detailed; includes operation of control surfaces etc.

'C' check Every 100 flying hours, as 'B'; but more searching; includes such items as fluid levels, lubrication checks etc.

'D' check Every 450 flying hours or 300 cycles; aircraft is brought into hangar, usually overnight, for more detailed maintenance.

'E' check Every 3,000 cycles or 15 months (in effect, annually, to avoid aircraft being unavailable during the summer months). Aircraft spends about two weeks out of service for thorough inspection. Any refurbishments to passenger accommodation are usually carried out at this time.

'F' check Every 6,000 cycles or 2 years } Progressively more
'G' check Every 12,000 cycles or 4 years } thorough examinations

N.B. Cycles are used rather than flying hours because of the short legs flown by many modern aircraft. Take-offs and landings are consequently the limiting factor.

Information supplied by Monarch Aircraft Engineering Ltd

the structure and the echo is collected. The type of echo received will reveal the presence of any defect. Electrical current is used in the eddy current system, utilising the fact that a small electric current will be disrupted by a flaw in its path, in this case the component being tested. A new testing technique uses thermal imagers, similar to those used by rescue workers to detect body heat, which are used to look over the outside of the aircraft's structure. Any tiny cracks will contain moisture, and this will reveal its presence by showing a temperature difference from that of the host metal.

Whilst these checks are carried out on the powerplants and airframe, diagnostic equipment is being used to vet the incredibly complex electrical and avionic systems, usually interfacing with test sockets fitted into the systems during manufacture. If any fault is found with the aircraft or its equipment, it is usual to replace the suspect component rather than repair it *in situ*. In this way the aircraft is detained for the minimum time, whilst technicians can work on the part in question in a workshop where conditions are better for specialised work. If the defective unit is capable of being repaired, it will be re-manufactured to as-new specification and returned to stores stock to await the next occasion when a replacement is called for.

These specialised workshops are often situated around the outside of the hangar and will deal with tasks such as engines, avionics and the hydraulic and pneumatic systems. Much of this work will, in the case of smaller operators, be returned to the equipment manufacturer or an engineering company which specialises in such repairs. In this way the capital cost of the necessary facilities can be avoided but, as ever, it boils down to a question of economics as to whether the work remains in-house or not.

The problem of corrosion receives much attention during servicing. All internal trim is removed periodically for the fuselage frame members to be inspected as, although the aircraft is fully treated during manufacture, this protection becomes less effective with time and use. The opportunity is sometimes taken to refurbish interior trim when it is out of the aircraft. The trim units are normally prefabricated for just such an eventuality, as it can be removed and replaced with relative ease, the replacement units again being units that have previously been reconditioned, again saving time on the maintenance period.

Very much allied to the prevention of corrosion is the process of painting aircraft; besides providing an advertisement for the carrier, the paint has a vital task in helping to combat corrosion. Aviation painting is carried out with great care: any carelessness in the preparation of the aircraft or the application of the finish could lead to it flaking or peeling in the harsh conditions of flight. The surface of the metal has to be meticulously prepared to provide a 'key' for the paint to bond with, and the paint — usually polyurethane — sprayed in conditions of great cleanliness. In addition, the painting area must be well ventilated and maintained at a constant temperature. For this reason the painting is carried out in a separate area of the maintenance centre where the noxious fumes produced by spray painting can be confined to minimise health hazards. The spray painters themselves work with masks, often supplied with breathing air from outside the paintshop.

Having painted the aircraft, operators must lavish a great deal of care on maintaining that finish. Again, a clean bright aircraft is a good advertisement, but cleanliness has another, more tangible benefit. A build-up of dirt on the highly-polished surface of an aircraft leads to a perceptible loss in performance and fuel economy, so regular cleaning is a necessity. Besides a regular washing down, each aircraft receives a thorough waxing from time to time: a 747 receives this every 12 weeks, and the operation takes 180 man-hours to complete, involving as it does nearly 1,700sq m of metal.

Hangars

The hangar itself is often a colossal structure costing millions of pounds. The need to provide a clear span (ie without supporting pillars) to accommodate the wingspan of a modern transport aircraft in safety, results in some very elegant structural engineering. Many hangar roofs are masterpieces of structural steelwork, resembling a series of bridges linked together to support the roof covering. Others employ steel cables for support, anchored to the ground outside the side walls. The access doors are always power operated, such is their great weight. The need to up-grade hangarage to accommodate new generation aircraft has led to the doors of some shorter hangars being replaced by 'tail docks' which wrap around the protruding tail of the aircraft under repair. The result is something akin to a gigantic Wellington boot!

Running beneath the hangar roof will often be an overhead crane, allowing large assemblies to be 'flown' over the floor as well as being used for working on aircraft, removing and refitting components. The problem of access for engineers is a thorny one, given the size of aircraft such as the 747. Some hangars incorporate tailor-made staging which closely follows the contours of the type being maintained, although this results in a loss of flexibility; it may not be a problem, however, if a fleet contains large numbers of one aircraft type. Using docks of this kind technicians can gain access to wings and upper fuselage by reaching from the staging. In a similar fashion a multi-storey structure is rolled around the tail unit, rather like the tail docks already described, but being open structures within the confines of the hangar. Where several types are maintained in the same bay a special dock cannot be easily employed, so free-standing work platforms are used, along with hydraulic platforms and 'scissors' lifts. Equipment of this type has an advantage in that it can be used in the open air for jobs not requiring covered accommodation.

The hangar floor will be well supplied with power points, both electric and pneumatic for portable tools and equipment, and a range of aircraft-compatible services to power systems under test without having to run either engines or APU. These services could well include hydraulic power, air-conditioning and 400Hz electric power besides both high and low pressure air; by using the low pressure air, engines can be run up on their starters to check oil systems and other ancillaries.

Major work on engines is often undertaken with them detached from the aircraft. With most present-day engines being in underwing pods (with the exception of tail engines in tri-jets), this job is not as daunting as it once was. Once the fastenings of the engine mountings are freed, the unit is lowered into a cradle which is towed into a specialised area for the necessary work to be carried out. When the work is completed, the engine can be tested in a test cell where it is securely anchored to a supporting structure. When connections for fuel, controls and instrumentation are made, the engine can be run up to its full power, the exhaust going into a silenced duct. Whilst in the cell, a full range of operating conditions can be simulated; the engine can, therefore, be fully tested and certified without being refitted on to the airframe.

The risk of fire is very high in areas where aircraft are maintained, where the presence of fuel and oil combined with activities such as welding poses a particular hazard. Whilst every precaution is taken to ensure safe working practices, extensive fire detection and fighting systems are installed. Detection systems often operate using two or more types of sensor: an infra-red detector, for instance, will produce a false alarm when it detects the flash from arc welding operations, whilst an ultra-violet sensor will not. The alarm will be raised, consequently, only when both infra-red and ultra-violet detectors agree that there is an abnormal situation.

Once the alarm has been raised, besides summoning the fire service the system will fight the fire automatically. The traditional roof sprinklers, although fitted, are of limited use if a fire has developed under the umbrella of an aircraft's wing. Should this be the case, foam will be discharged from the leading edges of the fixed dock, if one is fitted, or monitors installed at floor level. Besides the need to knock a fire down quickly, there is a conflicting requirement to contain any damage caused by the fire fighting itself. To this end, modern installations are capable of pinpointing a fire accurately within the vast area of the hangar and, having done that, focusing the sprinklers and monitors on just that area in the hope that water and foam damage can be kept to a minimum. There will also be a full complement of portable fire extinguishers and hose lines provided to supplement the fixed system and to tackle small fires on a first-aid basis.

Below:
Outdoor maintenance to a Boeing 757 of Monarch Airlines at Luton. *Author*

6 Airport Security and Emergency Services

Security

It is an unfortunate fact that the role of the airport security services, particularly that of the police, has changed significantly over recent years. Airports have always been the targets for crime, both petty and organised; the value of air cargo has made it an attractive subject for the criminal fraternity since the early days, whilst smuggling was a major industry in the years of strict currency controls following World War 2. Consequently, police and private security personnel have been on hand to try and counter such threats since the beginning of civil aviation.

Since the 1960s, however, air transport has been the focus of a far more sinister threat: that of politically motivated crime. The first hijack happened back in 1930, but the growth of civil air traffic has led to the situation where the aviation industry is extremely vulnerable to terrorist attack, be it in the form of hijacking, sabotage or ground attack. To combat this danger, British airports are the subject of the very tightest security.

The British government recognised the problem of terrorist crime many years ago and provisions to deal with it were incorporated into many of the Parliamentary Acts concerning civil aviation. These provisions were all consolidated into the 1982 Aviation Security Act, which gives the airport security services wide, and very necessary, powers to assist in the task of ensuring the safety of the public. Part of the Act places the duty of policing major airports in the hands of the local county or metropolitan police authority; for many years this has been undertaken by private security forces at many airports. In the 1970s, however, it was perceived that new problems of aviation security were getting beyond the resources of such a limited force, so the decision was made to include airport police within the framework of the local county or metropolitan force.

Although part of the county force, and under the command of the chief constable, the airport police are usually a separate unit whose officers are permanently detailed for airport duty. In this way they are able to know the airport, its staff and procedures intimately. The advantage of being part of a larger force lies in the ability to summon reinforcements and special services at short notice should an incident occur, and to be able to include off-airport areas in the planning for such an occasion.

The airport operator is obliged to pay a large part of the bill for the provision of these services, besides having to provide accommodation for them. In addition, it is responsible for providing passive security in the shape of fencing and access controls to the operational area. This fencing encloses the entire airside area and has uses in both stopping unauthorised entry and ensuring that all deplaning passengers and freight pass through customs and immigration controls. The security fence is, of course, very long and has to be patrolled regularly by the police to ensure its integrity; any break would immediately create an alert. Closed-circuit television and other electronic aids are also often used to supplement the standing patrols, and all gates are either fitted with alarms or manned by guards, usually employed by a private security organisation working for the airport authority on a contract basis. All staff and vehicles authorised to proceed airside are issued with security passes which are examined each time that a gate is passed through.

The airport police force operates its own police station within the airport complex and, bearing in mind that airports resemble small cities, spends much of its time dealing with the same sort of duties as any other police force, rather than the high profile airside duties. As a result, mundane tasks such as traffic duty, investigating minor crime and dealing with enquiries will form the 'base load' of their work.

As we have already seen, the first line of defence against any outside intervention is the security fence. The area within this is patrolled by police in 4×4 vehicles, usually Land Rover estate cars in radio contact with their own control and the ground movement controller in the tower. As these vehicles operate in the airport's active area, they must carry amber obstruction beacons in addition to their emergency blue lights. The officers undertaking these airside patrols must be alert for anyone trespassing on the airfield; anyone so found will certainly be detained and, most probably, charged. In the event of any incident involving terrorism, the airport police will be armed and will implement carefully formulated and rehearsed plans. Such plans are, of course, highly classified, but are likely to include the participation of various experts such as trained negotiators and marksmen.

Past exercises and alerts at Heathrow have involved the deployment of army units from the nearby barracks at Windsor; the author clearly remembers warily sharing the M4 motorway with a column of Scorpion light armoured vehicles, and mentally comparing their strength with that of the Morris Marina he was driving at the time!

The police would have a major role to play in the event of an aircraft emergency at the airport, as we will see later. The role would include traffic control, sealing the area from unauthorised entry and co-ordinating the various factions of the major incident plan.

Rescue and firefighting equipment and operations

Flying in a civil aircraft is one of the safest methods of getting from A to B; the civil aviation industry is so well regulated that nothing is left to chance. On the very rare occasions when things do go wrong, however, the potential for disaster is great indeed, as it is when any body leaves a state of rest. With aircraft the risk is created by horizontal speed and height, which in turn translates into vertical speed, and the fuel load carried by modern transports. These three factors conspire to create the situation where violent impact and fire could follow a loss of control.

Rescue and firefighting services (RFFS) are provided to intervene if a mishap occurs on or around the airfield; the granting of a licence to an airport operator is conditional on the provision of adequate RFFS, according to the type of traffic using the field. (The scale of RFFS categories is shown in Fig 18.) These categories determine the minimum facilities to be provided, although most airports exceed these minima by a substantial amount, using their experience to tailor services to local conditions. Heathrow, for example, is interesting in its provision of a small hovercraft to help deal with any incident involving the neighbouring Perry Oaks water treatment plant.

The resulting airport fire service is organised very much along the lines of the local authority fire brigades (LAFB), but is a unit dedicated to react quickly to

Fig 18 Aerodrome category for firefighting and rescue		
Aerodrome category	Aircraft overall length	Maximum fuselage width
1	up to but not including 9m	2m
2	9m up to but not including 12m	2m
3	12m up to but not including 18m	3m
4	18m up to but not including 24m	4m
5	24m up to but not including 28m	4m
6	28m up to but not including 39m	5m
7	39m up to but not including 49m	5m
8	49m up to but not including 61m	7m
9	61m up to but not including 76m	7m

aviation emergencies on, and immediately around, the airfield and is funded by the airport authority. It maintains very close links with the LAFB as, in the case of an incident, they would operate side by side — the county brigade providing essential reinforcement and re-supply. The personnel employed on airport fire duties have to meet the same medical criteria as their local authority colleagues and use much of the same equipment, ensuring compatibility between the two services.

The CAA sets very strict targets for airport RFFS: an appliance must be able to reach either end of the main runway within three minutes of receiving an alarm, for instance. That three minutes includes the time taken for the crew to board their appliance, so it is a very demanding response time. In the case of a very large airfield such as Heathrow, a second fire station is provided to meet the three-minute rule; in a situation such as this the number of appliances required for the RFFS category can be split between the two stations. The response time stipulations necessitate the use of fire appliances with really excellent performance; the CAA regulations require a 0-50 acceleration in 40sec and a top speed of 62mph for the largest appliances, which weigh about 30 tons each. Not bad going!

There are three basic types of airport fire appliance: the rapid intervention vehicle (RIV), the light foam tender and the heavy foam tender. All these share some common design features, namely all-wheel drive to ensure good off-road mobility, and good stability. The CAA stipulates that the machine must be capable of tilting to a chassis angle of 33° without toppling. The other common feature is that all appliances carry large quantities of firefighting medium to attack the raging fuel fires that could follow an incident.

The RIV is the smallest, lightest appliance used by the RFFS, and is used by them to spearhead any rescue effort. Because of the ferocity of an aircraft fire, time is of the absolute essence; in a smoke-filled cabin, seconds can make the difference between the occupants being survivors or victims. As a result of this the RIV is designed to reach the incident scene in the shortest time possible; it must have a top speed of 65mph or above

and be capable of reaching 50mph in 25sec or less. To achieve performance of this order sacrifices have to be made in the amount of equipment and firefighting medium carried. The regulations call for a minimum of 900 litres (200gal) of water, plus foam concentrate. Although this appears to be a small amount, it is adequate for the role of the vehicle, ie that of holding any fire down until the major vehicles attend, usually only seconds later. The prime purpose of rapid intervention is to secure the escape route for survivors; the RIV will make for the area where escape is possible or actually taking place, and attack the fire in that limited area. If possible, the crew will assist in the evacuation of the aircraft, but care must be taken so as not to obstruct any escape routes already in use.

The equipment carried on these vehicles varies from airport to airport, but will always include 'fire extinguishing medium' as mentioned above. The 'medium' specified in the CAA regulations is usually foam, but the use of dry powder or halocarbons is allowed. These halocarbons are liquids (often abbreviated to 'halons') which vaporise when sprayed on to a fire, the resulting vapour excluding oxygen and smothering it. The most common halon is BCF (Bromochlorodifluoromethane); whatever the medium, it is delivered by either hoses, known as hand lines or side lines, or by a monitor, essentially a water cannon mounted on the cab roof or front bumper. Many RIVs use a pump driven via a power take-off (PTO) from the main engine; others employ a tank filled with pre-mixed water and foam which is pressurised immediately before use. The pressure is provided by gas — be it carbon dioxide, nitrogen or compressed air — stored in bottles installed on the appliance. The RIVs at Luton use this system to deliver foam to a bumper-mounted monitor which is remotely controlled, along with hand lines. The use of compressed gas as a propellant in such a case gives the advantage of greater simplicity than a pump, with its associated PTO and controls, but suffers from the handicap of not being capable of replenishment at the incident scene as the tank would lose all its pressure if opened. This handicap is not significant to an RIV, however, as by the time the tank has been discharged the major units would be in attendance, taking over the responsibility for the firefighting effort.

Rescue equipment may be carried on the RIV, on a major appliance or, occasionally, on a specialised emergency tender. Such equipment is, yet again, subject to CAA minima and includes such items as ladders, axes and power tools to help effect an entry into an aircraft.

Chassis types used for rapid intervention vehicles vary because of conditions at the airport where they are stationed. A common base vehicle for RIV use is a Range Rover, stretched from 4×4 to 6×4 configuration by adding a third, unpowered axle and lengthening the chassis. (In terms such as 4×4 and 6×4, the first figure denotes the total number of road wheels, whilst the second relates to the number which are powered.) A typical Range Rover RIV carries 200gal of pre-mixed water and foam, fed by a front-mounted pump to a roof-mounted monitor, along with a 100kg BCF installation. Such is the power and mobility of the Range Rover that it still has excellent performance, both on and off the road, when used at this weight.

A similar, though slightly larger, vehicle is the Stonefield 6×4, a forward control unit built at Strood in Kent, which uses a 5.3 litre V8 petrol engine to give the requisite performance. A number of American 4×4s such as Jeep, Dodge and Chevrolet can be seen in use at smaller airports.

Airports in the higher RFFS categories often have need of an RIV with greater foam capacity than the CAA minimum. This need results in the use of larger vehicles such as the Reynolds Boughton Apollo-based machines at Luton airport. This chassis, rated at 5.5 tons GVW, uses a Chevrolet V8 petrol engine delivering no less than 195bhp. With a power/weight ratio of over 35bhp/ton it is not surprising that these vehicles are lively performers! The Luton RIVs, along with other Apollos of the same age, could easily be mistaken for Ford products as the chassis is a heavily modified Ford 'A' series, including the original cab. Upon the demise of the 'A' series, Reynolds Boughton switched to using the Renault/Dodge 50 series as the starting point for the Apollo. Again the chassis is extensively modified for its new role, these modifications including the fitting of a Rolls-Royce V8 petrol engine.

The line between the RIV and the light foam tender (LFT) is a blurred one. Some airports now use a LFT in the rapid intervention role where their increased foam capacity allows a longer period of firefighting. In such cases the performance criteria for RIVs apply. The fitting of a full-scale foam system means that the LFT can be supplied with water from outside sources, hydrants or a supporting appliance, for instance, allowing them to remain active for a far greater time.

A typical LFT is the Gloster-Saro Meteor, used by the BAA, amongst others. The Meteor is powered by a rear-mounted Detroit two-stroke diesel driving through an automatic gearbox to all four wheels; the mid-mounted pump is driven by a PTO sandwiched between the engine and gearbox which allows the tender to be driven slowly without interrupting the delivery of foam from the pump. Being larger than a pure RIV, the LFT can carry a greater range of rescue equipment along with a larger quantity of water and foam, commonly about 6,000 litres of water plus foam concentrate. The BAA Meteors are fitted with a monitor on the front bumper besides hand lines wound on to reels in the side lockers, allowing foam to be brought to bear in the minimum possible time.

At the top of the RFFS range is the major foam tender (MFT). These magnificent machines are invariably mounted on a 6×6 chassis in the UK, although 8×8 units are to be found overseas. Modern units are rear-engined, this helping to keep noise levels in the cab down to a reasonable level, and nearly always have a central driving position. The Gloster-Saro Javelin is used as a MFT by many airports, including the BAA group and Luton. Operating at about 30 tons GVW, these machines are still capable of reaching 50mph in less than 40sec and have a maximum speed of over 60mph — and all this whilst carrying between 10,000 and 12,000 litres of water plus foam concentrate. The high performance is achieved by fitting a huge Detroit two-stroke engine, developing well over 500bhp, which transmits its power to all six wheels through an automatic gearbox.

The foam system is centred around a mid-mounted pump which incorporates an automatic foam-metering device to ensure that the correct ratio of foam concentrate to water is maintained under all operating conditions. The power of the pumping equipment is such that 10,000gal/min of foam can be produced; this output is delivered by the MFT's main weapon, the rooftop monitor. This equipment is able to project foam up to a distance of 60m from the tender with great force and accuracy. The monitor is usually power-operated on modern appliances to counteract the reaction from the nozzle, and is capable of being controlled from within the cab. The UK regulations, however, forbid the driver from performing this duty so the operator usually stands on a platform behind the cab and manipulates the controls from this position. Bearing in mind that the total water capacity can be exhausted in two minutes, it is vital that foam is applied accurately, as wastage could deplete the firefighting effort significantly.

On the nozzle of the monitor is a diffuser, shaped like a fishtail, which can be closed over the stream of foam to produce a flat, wide spray pattern suitable for covering large areas of fire. For obvious reasons, this fitting is colloquially known as a 'blabbermouth'.

A self-protection system can be installed on most appliances, comprising water sprays fitted around the body to counter radiant heat and foam nozzles beneath the vehicle to lay a carpet of foam so that the tender can advance over burning fuel. Although the unit can advance closer to a fire, it is at the cost of increased weight, as any water and foam carried for this purpose must be in addition to the CAA minimum amounts for RFFS purposes. In the case of a localised fire breaking out in an aircraft engine, a 'complementary medium' will be used to attack it. This medium could be dry powder, carbon dioxide (CO_2) or BFC (Halon), the latter being the most common. Most major foam tenders, and many smaller ones, carry a BFC installation comprising the liquid along with a gas propellant (usually CO_2 or nitrogen) which is fired into the liquid tank to pressurise it, like a giant aerosol. Halons are used only in areas with good ventilation as the fumes produced can be toxic in enclosed spaces; but, in the right circumstances, they are capable of knocking a fire down very quickly. For this reason they are employed for engine fires as, hopefully, their early use can stop fire spreading to the main structure of the aircraft. A further benefit of halons is that

they do not conduct electricity, so are very useful for tackling fires in electrical and electronic equipment.

An example of aviation technology leading to changes in land-based procedures can be seen clearly with reference to the subject of engine fires. The tail-mounted engines in TriStar and DC-10 transports require a special means of access by airport fire services. As a result of this many MFTs mount a hydraulically-operated ladder, similar to a miniature turntable ladder, which can extend to over 30ft from the ground. As it has a built-in halon supply this device allows fires in these high mounted engines to be tackled much more easily, besides being available as a conventional escape ladder to assist in evacuation.

Auxiliary power on an MFT is provided in the form of a 110V electrical supply and compressed air. Power rescue tools can be operated by either of these means, whilst the 110V supply is, in addition, used to power remotely-controlled 500W floodlights mounted on a telescopic mast capable of being elevated to 25ft above the ground. This is essential at airports where 24hr operations take place, as the confusion resulting from a night-time incident can be lessened by the provision of first-rate lighting.

Although the CAA regulations call for the provision of MFTs of a type similar to the Javelin, many examples of the previous generation of foam tenders can still be seen at airports, fulfilling second line duties. The machines are usually based on a Thornycroft Nubian Major chassis — again a 6×6 design — but with a front-mounted engine. Although the Nubian Major is no longer 'state of the art', it is still a formidable fire appliance, held in high esteem by the crews who operate it. Whilst its performance is now below the required minima, it is, nevertheless, capable of producing 6,500gal of foam per minute.

Besides the vehicles provided to fulfil the licensing requirements, many airports have other units on hand to cope with local conditions. A common provision is a foam tanker, carrying bulk supplies of foam concentrate to replenish the tanks of the MFTs (which must, in any case, carry enough concentrate to mix with twice their water capacity). Personnel carriers and general-purpose vehicles — often Land Rovers — are generally available,

Above:
Gloster Saro RIV on a Range Rover 6×4 chassis. *Gloster Saro*

Below:
This RIV stationed at Luton Airport is based on a Reynolds Boughton 'Apollo' chassis.
Clearly visible is the remotely controlled monitor mounted on the front bumper.
Author

Above left:
The Gloster Saro 'Protector' light foam tender.   *Gloster Saro*

Left:
Gloster Saro's 'Meteor' light foam tender provides first-strike protection at Gatwick.
Gloster Saro

Below left:
Also in use at Gatwick is the Gloster Saro 'Javelin' major foam tender. Note the monitor
on the cab roof with its fan-shaped diffuser. Behind this is the hydraulic escape.
Gloster Saro

Above:
Luton Airport's fire station shows (left to right) Thornycroft Nubian Major, two Javelins
and an RIV.   *Author*

Below:
Rescue and firefighting techniques being practised at Luton Airport using the fuselage
of a Britannia. In the background can be seen the airport's approach lighting, mounted
on masts owing to the steep drop at the end of the runway.   *Author*

Above and below:
The work of the CAA's Fire Service Training School at Tees-side Airport.   *CAA*

whilst less common vehicles include emergency tenders and mobile control units.

The local authority fire brigade may also base specialised appliances in the area of an airport, both to assist the RFFS with an incident on the field and to cope with an aircraft incident in the surrounding area. In the latter case, the airport emergency services would react in a limited manner if the incident was within a defined radius of the airport. The LAFB will often base a foam tender at the nearest fire station to the airport along with, perhaps, a hose layer. These hose layers carry large quantities of hose, already coupled and laid zig-zag fashion in the body, ready to be drawn out of the vehicle as it drives towards the scene of the fire.

As in the case of the county fire brigade, the airport RFFS keeps up its level of expertise by constant training. Airports usually have their own practice wreck where firefighting and rescue techniques can be perfected. This poor beast is doused in kerosene from time to time for the firemen to practice in the use of foam, whilst the interior can be filled with smoke so that breathing apparatus can be used and the sensation of operating in zero visibility experienced. Airport firemen are awarded certificates of competency by the CAA at various levels of skill. Formal training to reach these levels is given by the CAA at its Fire Service Training School at Teesside Airport. This world-famous establishment can boast a full range of facilities including smoke chambers, practice aircraft and modern fire appliances, along with the associated lecture rooms and student accommodation. BAA maintains its own training school, approved by the CAA, for training its own personnel as well as other firefighters on an agency basis.

'On job' training continues on a daily basis: RFFS crews must be thoroughly familiar with their airfields and their surroundings, along with the routes to any possible incident. At some airports the fire service personnel have other, non-emergency tasks — winter maintenance for instance. By being out and about on the airport (but always in radio contact with their control room) they are always up to date with any changes taking place, and get to know the people with whom they would work in an emergency — the airfield ATC for example. In a similar way there are frequent joint exercises with the LAFB so that both services will be familiar with each other's procedures and equipment.

It is also beholden on the RFFS to make themselves familiar with the layout of all aircraft operating in and out of the airport. This is particularly important as significant differences can exist even between aircraft of the same type. This familiarity is gained by reading manufacturers' data sheets, which are published for the purpose, and by looking over actual aircraft as they visit the field. Reminder cards are often prepared by the firemen themselves and carried in the cab of the tender, these cards covering such features as the method of operating exits, position of electrical master switches and the location of pressure bottles which could become a hazard in the heat of a fire.

Medical services

In contrast to the elaborate RFFS provisions, airport medical services are often fairly simple, relying heavily on the intervention of the local county ambulance services in the case of an emergency. There will, however, be a supply of medical equipment available, along with people competent in its use. Where the airport maintains a full-time medical service this will be called out but, in all cases, the fire crews will be fully trained in first aid. Equipment must be available in relation to the RFFS category of the airport, this including medical packs, foil blankets, resuscitators and stretchers. This equipment is sometimes carried on a special vehicle which may also carry tents to accommodate casualties awaiting removal by ambulance. Luton Airport provides two inflatable igloos, kept inflated by petrol-driven fans and carried on an ex-RIV Range Rover. There is, perhaps surprisingly, no obligation for an airport to operate an ambulance unless the county ambulance service would take more than 15min to attend.

The system in action

Having looked at the components of the rescue and firefighting services, it might be interesting to follow the course of an imaginary incident.

The first inkling of trouble that the rescue and firefighting services receive will be from one of several sources: in the rare event of a pilot declaring an in-flight emergency, it will be the NATCC that alerts the airport control tower that the stricken aircraft is being directed to them. The tower will alert its RFFS, which will normally have the time, in this event, to position its apppliances along the runway ready to deal with the emergency.

In most incidents, however, the airport authorities do not have the luxury of time. As most trouble occurs during take-off or landing, the aircraft involved is under the control of the aerodrome controllers; it is they, therefore, who will normally sound the initial alarm, having received a distress call from the pilot or having lost radar contact with the aircraft. Information may also come in from the police as a result of 999 calls from the public. Most airport fire stations have a watchroom overlooking the operational area, similar to a small control tower, and the duty officers will be able to see for themselves if a crisis is developing. The watchroom also monitors the aerodrome ATC frequencies so it will also hear any distress call and will react before the alarm is transmitted from the tower, often saving vital seconds.

In any case, the fire appliances will be turned out at high speed upon hearing the alarm, which will be followed up by a message from the tower giving aircraft type, number of passengers and estimated location of the casualty. At some airports the RFFS vehicles can be guided from their station to the incident by means of the switchable taxiway lighting (**see Chapter 7**), whilst an interesting provision at Gatwick allows the tower to set the signals on the nearby London to Brighton railway line to 'danger' if an incident occurs in the area.

As the rescue crews race to the scene, often receiving further details by radio telephone en route, the emergency plan will be swinging into action and many things happening simultaneously. The airport ATC, having told ATCC of its plight, will be urgently redirecting all incoming traffic away from its own field. ATCC will have to feed this traffic to neighbouring establishments, provided that they are able to handle it; if not it will be directed to the nearest suitable site, the passengers finishing their journeys by internal flights or surface transport. At the same time the duty officer at the airport fire station will be talking to his LAFB opposite number via direct telephone line between the two controls, giving him whatever details he has to hand.

This will put a predetermined level of response into effect, with surrounding county fire stations directing pumps and special appliances to the airport. Around every airport will be seen roadsigns bearing the legend 'RVP', often followed by a compass bearing (eg Heathrow has RVP N, NW, W, S, SE and E, whilst Luton just has the one RVP). These RVPs are the rendezvous points, used by the airport to direct publc emergency services to the point nearest to the incident, where they will be met by one of the guide vehicles with their 'follow me' signs. This guidance is vital because, at the time of the incident, aircraft may have been taxiing out and these will need to be brought back to the terminal. For this reason the incoming emergency vehicles need to move under the guidance of the ground movements controller, via the airport's guide vehicles.

During these first seconds of the emergency the alert will be spreading far and wide. The county ambulance service will be sending every possible unit to the airport, again being advised of the relevant RVP. Under the terms of the major incident plan, all non-emergency ambulance work will be postponed whilst area hospitals will be warned to expect casualties, each hospital declaring how many it will be able to take, if necessary. The police force will also be implementing its response, with the airport division in the forefront, securing the incident site and aiding the rescue work. The traffic division, meanwhile, will be rushing to the scene to control traffic in favour of emergency vehicles. A mobile police control room will also be dispatched.

The waves from this major incident plan reach very far; adjoining county fire brigades will be moving in to cover gaps left by the response to the alert, whilst organisations such as the Red Cross and St John Ambulance Brigade will be notified. Military authorities may well be put on standby, as their assistance could be called for.

To return to the airport: within the statutory 3min the RFFS will be on the scene, the RIVs or LFTs arriving first. We will assume that 'our' casualty aircraft has landed short of the threshold, its undercarriage collapsing and a fuel fire starting — not an unimaginable set of circumstances. In this case the first strike appliances will approach from upwind so as to be clear of smoke, using their sirens continuously as there could be dazed survivors in the area. If there are to be survivors, the aircraft will have to be largely evacuated by this time. Once the aircraft has come to rest, the cabin crew will be working frantically to clear passengers from the aircraft: seconds really do count in this situation. The cabin crew are extensively trained in this duty; indeed, it is largely the reason that they are there. In an emergency there is likely to be total confusion: some passengers may panic whilst others may be rooted to the spot by fear. Every possible means must be used by the crew to get everyone out of the doors and emergency exits before any fire takes hold; it is during these first seconds that an incident can become a disaster.

A system currently under development by a UK company, and known by the acronym SAVE (Safety Aircraft and Vehicles Equipment), seeks to prolong the survival time by fitting three rows of sprinklers along the cabin ceiling. Following an incident, on-board water (including galley water supplies) is pumped by a nitrogen-powered pump through the centre row of sprinklers, producing a water mist. For a medium-sized transport, 15gal of water per minute will wash smoke and toxic gases out of the atmosphere at the same time as absorbing heat. Forty-five gallons of water is, therefore, sufficient to protect the cabin until the arrival of the rescue services; at this point they will connect one of their tenders to a coupling on the outside of the aircraft and proceed to pump water through the two rows of sprinklers under the luggage racks, deluging the cabin interior. Recent test at Teesside Airport showed that the system held the interior temperature down to 90°C when a fuel fire reaching 1,400°C had been started outside, whilst visibility stayed acceptable and the atmosphere remained breathable. International manufacturers and aviation authorities are reported to be very impressed with the system, but foolproof precautions will need to be incorporated to prevent accidental discharge which could cause critical damage to the aircraft's electrical and electronic systems.

Until such time as a system of this type becomes a reality, the time available for escape remains limited, so evacuation remains the overriding priority. The crews of the first appliance to arrive will work to keep escape routes safe by suppressing any fire in the area of the exits and, if circumstances permit, opening up further escape routes. All aircraft have emergency windows which can be removed and areas marked on the fuselage where rescue workers can cut into the fuselage without the risk of cutting electric cables or pressurised pipes; bearing in mind the limited time available, however, such options are limited.

Very shortly after this initial response, the major foam tenders will arrive. They will attack the main seat of the fire using their monitors to deliver the huge quantities of foam needed, a priority being to beat the fire back from the fuselage. Therefore at least one tender will concentrate on applying copious amounts of foam along the wing root and fuselage side, whilst others concentrate on knocking down the fire in the surrounding area. The main effort at all times is rescue: any initial firefighting only takes place to protect life, and only when the aircraft is evacuated will any effort be put into saving it as a piece of hardware.

The major foam tenders will exhaust their on-board supplies of water within a few minutes, so the aim is to have the fire well under control in that time. Before those few minutes have elapsed, the local authority fire and ambulance services should both be starting to arrive. Once at the scene, the role of the ambulance service is clear: to remove casualties from the area as quickly and efficiently as possible. It is probable that all survivors will be suffering from a certain degree of shock and the effects of smoke, therefore everyone is likely to be taken to hospital. There could be a delay in getting sufficient ambulances to the scene; indeed, they will probably operate a shuttle service to and from the casualty departments of local hospitals. Shelters are often provided to house survivors pending transport. In the event of large numbers of uninjured survivors, however, the emergency plan may include the use of the airport's buses for transport to either a hospital or an area of the airport earmarked for use as a casualty station. Doctors and nurses from the area accident rescue team will be in attendance quickly, bringing specialised skills and equipment; the county ambulance service's major incident vehicle will also be dispatched, carrying large quantities of such items as stretchers and blankets to supplement the airport's own stock. Part of the emergency plan should also provide for emotional support for survivors, given by those with counselling skills such as a local clergymen and the Salvation Army.

The task of the county fire brigade is a complex one, and will vary with the circumstances of the incident. If the aircraft is not evacuated by the time of their arrival, the LAFB crews wearing breathing apparatus will enter the cabin, if possible, and institute a search for further survivors. A hose with a water fog nozzle would often be introduced in an attempt to control the cabin temperature, but may already have been deployed by the airport RFFS, perhaps by breaking windows. It is very important for the rescuers to make a new entrance if they are entering the cabin before it is evacuated, as the conflict of movement in the doorways must be avoided at all costs. The other main priority of the LAFB, if the fire is still alight, is to take urgent steps to re-supply the airport's own brigade with water and to intervene themselves.

Water supplies vary from airport to airport: some major airports have a ring main installed alongside the runways and taxiways, and hydrants can be coupled into this in the same way as in a street.

Other airports use large storage tanks sited around the field. The LAFB couples up to a hydrant, or uses a suction hose to lift water from the storage tank and relays it to the airport appliances; the use of standard hose and couplings ensures compatibility. In this situation, the use of a hose-layer is often called for as the distances involved may be too great for manual hose-laying. Consideration is being given at some locations to providing an ex-fuel company refuelling tanker, modified for use as a mobile bulk water supply. Although such a vehicle has very poor off-road mobility, it could be driven to the nearest hard standing and then used to supply appliances involved on the fire ground.

All this has taken some time to describe on paper, but in reality events would happen very, very quickly. The severity of an aircraft fuel fire does not allow the wastage of a single second, and all the personnel and equipment involved in RFFS have that end in view. After an incident there would be a very thorough debriefing of all the parties involved. This would parallel the investigation into the cause of the mishap by the Accidents Investigation Branch of the Department of Transport, involving specialists in the fields of engineering, air traffic control procedures and other fields of aviation knowledge. These investigations could result in changes in procedures and equipment in the light of hard-won experience. The fact that this experience is used profitably is typical of the care taken over the whole field of civil aviation safety.

Below:
Based at Norwich Airport, this major foam tender is unusual in the UK, being based on a Mercedes-Benz 6×6 chassis. *Gloster Saro*

7 Airport Navigation Services

When examined objectively, the mechanics of getting a 747 on to the ground safely are very impressive indeed. After flying for maybe thousands of miles this 350-ton monster is expected to put its wheels down on just the correct part of a strip of ground no more than 4km long and 45m wide, at over 150mph and in the worst of weather. The fact that, in the UK alone, this happens thousands of times a day without incident, is a testimony to the absolute reliability of the system.

The levels of navigation equipment provided at an airport largely determine the visibility minima that apply and, therefore, its category. These categories are laid down in the UK by the CAA, and are defined on page 104. The electronic navigational aids (navaids) that allow an airfield to operate in Category III are very costly, but a balance must be struck between this cost and the benefits that accrue from being able to receive suitably equipped aircraft in almost zero visibility. Whilst most airfield navaids are installed to meet statutory requirements, other equipment may be provided to help ease the workload of the control staff, thereby allowing increased traffic levels to be handled.

Control tower

The air traffic controllers on duty in the control tower are, in effect, the first and last links in a chain stretching around the world — this chain being the international air traffic control system. Their duty **(see Chapter 1)** is to receive traffic bound for their airport from the Air Traffic Control Centre (ATCC) and handle it during the final stages, not relinquishing that control until the chocks go under the wheels and main power is shut down. At the other extreme this control extends from before engine start until the aircraft is climbing out, at which time the flight will be handed back to ATCC, and back into the global system.

The most visible component of the air traffic control (ATC) system is the control tower, which can vary in sophistication in relation to the intensity of operations to be dealt with. At a large airport, the tower's functions will be divided into different sections, each handling a particular portion of the landing or take-off phases. The controllers who deal with the flight first do not actually see an aircraft at all whilst on duty. These are the approach controllers, who use radar to regulate incoming traffic and to establish it on to the correct approach for the runway in use.

Radar

A busy airport such as Heathrow or Gatwick could not operate at its traffic levels without the use of radar in several functions — such as traffic regulation — in addition to the obvious primary use for collision avoidance.

The two broad types of radar are primary and secondary: primary radar depicts 'raw' data — basically traces of aircraft along with permanent echoes from ground features such as hills or buildings. These permanent echoes can, however, be eliminated for the sake of clarity by the use of special circuitry which only shows traces which move between one sweep of the plot and the next. This type of radar is known as a moving target indicator. The problem with the raw data presented on the primary radar screen is that the controller is faced with masses of echoes, not knowing which is which. This was also a problem in World War 2 when operators could not distinguish between enemy aircraft and defending fighters; consequently a device known as IFF (Identification Friend or Foe) was fitted to allied aircraft. This device, when triggered by a suitable radar signal, transmitted a code back to be displayed on the plot, thus identifying the aircraft. It was this system that formed the basis of SSR

(Secondary Surveillance Radar), the main tool of the ATC system.

SSR relies on the active 'co-operation' of the aircraft's electronic system which, like IFF, transmits coded information back to the ground along with its echo. This information is received by a second antenna, often located above the primary radar head. The data comprises a four-figure code — the flight's 'squawk' — a code entered into the aircraft's transponder by the pilot on the instructions of ATC. Along with this code is transmitted the altitude, culled directly from the altimeter and, when it reaches the ATCC a blink later, it is processed so that it appears alongside the aircraft's echo on the plot. Thus the flight will be positively identified, as the 'squawk' will have been processed into a flight number along with its current altitude and a route code, also computer generated. An alarm function displays a distress symbol in the case of an in-flight emergency being declared by the pilot.

SSR is obviously far more useful than primary radar and is used for the national ATC function, gathering information from a number of radar heads located around the country. The echoes from these units are synchronised by a computer system in the ATCC. In the case of Heathrow, the alphanumeric information from the London ATCC is added to the airport's own primary radar to give an SSR for approach control.

In addition to approach radar, many airports will use a surveillance radar for preliminary guidance to inbound flights as well as exit guidance for departures. A further function is the en route radar information service for aircraft overflying the airport's area.

In the Visual Control Room (VCR) there may be a repeater of the approach radar, known as the Distance From Touchdown Indicator (DFTI). Rather than showing a full 360°, this instrument displays only the segment of the main plot of interest to the air arrivals controller, who will be able to see the sequence of incoming flights from the SSR information displayed. By adding range marks, the controller is able to assess the distance from the threshold with accuracy.

Another radar which is becoming increasingly common at modern airports is the Airfield Surface Movement Indicator (ASMI). It displays what amounts to

a map of the airfield showing the position of aircraft using the runways and taxiways along with vehicles operating on the field. The head of this radar revolves at a high speed and produces a high resolution plot which is used by various controllers, such as the air approach controller, his ground movements colleague and the assistant regulating the lighting.

Radio and telecommunications

Of related interest is the airport's range of radio communications facilities. All airports are allocated at least two radio frequencies: an approach control frequency and one for the tower. In addition, many airports have a ground movements radio operating, like the two above, on Very High Frequency (VHF), whilst control of vehicles will be via Ultra High Frequency (UHF) channels. Heathrow can boast a total of 14 VHF channels for ground/air communications and 11 UHF channels for ground/ground use. Each VHF facility has duplicate and, sometimes, triplicate transmitter/receivers for standby use. The UHF channels are used to provide control over ground services such as airport maintenance crews, snow operations and the airport emergency services. Some of these channels are linked to VHF so that a controller can communicate with both aircraft and vehicles simultaneously.

A further aid to approach controllers is Digital Resolution Direction Finder (DRDF) which automatically displays a magnetic bearing from the airport to the aircraft communicating with the control position.

Besides the above speech channels, large airports operate Automated Terminal Information Service (ATIS) which continuously transmits essential data such as runway in use, weather, navaid status and so on. These transmissions are continuously updated, and each bulletin is assigned a code letter starting with 'alpha' and progressing to 'zulu'. This letter is given by the pilot of an incoming flight, having copied the ATIS details previously, to the approach controller to prove that he is in possession of the most up-to-date details. Departure ATIS is similarly provided at some airports for aircrew to copy before commencing their departure routine.

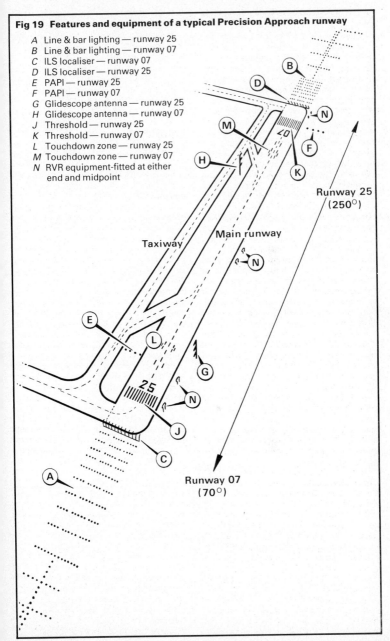

Fig 19 Features and equipment of a typical Precision Approach runway

- A Line & bar lighting — runway 25
- B Line & bar lighting — runway 07
- C ILS localiser — runway 07
- D ILS localiser — runway 25
- E PAPI — runway 25
- F PAPI — runway 07
- G Glidescope antenna — runway 25
- H Glidescope antenna — runway 07
- J Threshold — runway 25
- K Threshold — runway 07
- L Touchdown zone — runway 25
- M Touchdown zone — runway 07
- N RVR equipment-fitted at either end and midpoint

Runway 25 (250°)

Taxiway

Main runway

Runway 07 (70°)

Every airport is also connected to other aviation establishments by comprehensive land communications links. These links connect all airports and control centres by a system of private speech and data circuits to provide reliable, swift connection. The main switching centre for the Aeronautical Fixed Telecommunications Network (AFTN) is in the tower at Heathrow, and it is here that the UK's network interfaces with the worldwide system. Weather details, notices to airmen (NOTAMs) and flight plans are amongst the traffic carried by AFTN, which routinely passes 100,000 messages per day through Heathrow. The UK domestic system is the Administrative Telephone Network (ATN) which links users all over the country via exchanges at Heathrow, Manchester and Prestwick.

Landing aids

The business end of all this wizardry is the control tower itself, the nerve centre of any airport. The public perception of the control tower is that all stages of the flight are handled from there; this is, of course, not the case as once away from the airport's control zone, all traffic is controlled by the Air Traffic Control Centres (ATCCs) at West Drayton in Middlesex and Prestwick in Scotland. Once handed over by the ATCC, the safety of the flight rests with the airport's own ATC system. At many airports these services are provided on a contract basis by the National Air Traffic Services division of the CAA whilst at others, controllers are employed directly by the airport operator. In the latter case, the controllers must be licensed by the CAA in the same way as their own employees.

As mentioned before, a major control tower is divided into two distinct operational areas: the approach control and the visual control room. The approach controller, as we saw in Chapter 1, takes the incoming flight from the ATCC. He will, however, have been warned of the flight's arrival by a flight progress strip, received from ATCC via a printer connected to their computer. The flight strip is generated from information given on the flight plan, filed before the flight starts. These flight plans are stored in the computer's memory in the case of regular flights which follow the same routeings and timings.

As the flight reports in, the flight progress strip will be taken and slotted into the top of a rack, thereby establishing it in the sequence of arrivals. As each flight is handed off to aerodrome control, its strip is taken out of the 'live' rack, every strip above dropping down one space. Whilst under a controller's jurisdiction, all instructions issued to a flight are marked on the strip as an *aide-mémoire* to the controller, and as potential evidence in the event of an incident. Audio tapes of all radio and telephone conversations are recorded and kept for 30 days for the same reason.

The scene of activity moves up to the VCR when the flight is between six and eight miles from touchdown. The VCR is most people's picture of the control tower; this is the most visible part of the ATC, perched as it is way above the rest of the airfield. In the VCR are the air arrivals controller and ground movements con-

Fig 20 Instrument Landing System (ILS)

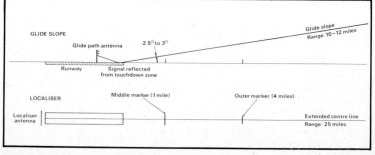

troller, along with perhaps other controllers and assistants at busy airports. These assistants' duties include updating flight progress strips and controlling the airfield lighting.

During this phase of the approach the aircraft will have established on the Instrument Landing System (ILS), which is now an invaluable aid to safe airport operation. As with many other present day navaids, ILS grew from a navigation system developed during World War 2, in this case a German blind bombing system called Knickebein. ILS comprises two beams: a localiser which operates at VHF giving horizontal guidance, and a UHF beam defining the glidepath. In addition there are two marker beacons along the runway's extended centre line, known as fan markers, owing to their transmission pattern. The localiser aerial can be seen at the upwind end of the runway and looks like a large yellow fence, and the glideslope aerial is a mast situated at the downwind end. Each component functions independently, but when interpreted by an aircraft's instruments, combine to provide accurate guidance down to a height where the pilot can land using visual means, or even below that height if the runway and aircraft have full autoland capability.

Using ILS an aircraft will acquire the localiser signal as it turns on to the extended centre line under the instructions of the approach controller. The guidance offered by the ILS will either be fed directly into the autopilot or one of a variety of flight instruments, from which the pilot will fly the landing manually. The former is known as a coupled approach. As the localiser has a range of about 25 miles against the glideslope's 10, there is a phase of the approach where the pilot is receiving horizontal reference only; he receives instructions regarding his altitude from the approach controller. At about 10 miles the glideslope beam will activate the vertical component of either the autopilot or instruments, and the aircraft flies down the glideslope at a uniform 3°. At four nautical miles out the outer marker will be crossed, its passage being marked by the audible tone in the crews' headphones. This is used as a reporting point by ATC and, shortly after, at one nautical mile, the middle marker is crossed denoting the final phase of the landing.

If the aircraft has been executing a coupled approach, the pilot should now disengage the autopilot if he has the approach lighting in view. The co-pilot normally handles the controls during the instrument phase, allowing the pilot to keep a lookout for the lighting, so saving the need to re-focus his eyes after looking within the cockpit. In the case of a full autolanding, the ILS will fly the aircraft right down on to the runway by providing inputs to both the autopilot and autothrottle. By receiving data from a radio altimeter, the autoland will flare the aircraft on to the runway. Airlines tend to impose their own visibility minima above that of the system as an additional safeguard. In practice, however, a suitably equipped aircraft could land on a compatible runway in virtually zero visibility.

Although ILS is in universal use, a long-term replacement is being developed in the shape of the Microwave Landing System (MLS). This system has better resistance to interference and can provide guidance within a funnel, up to 40° on either side of the extended centre line. This has the potential for allowing incoming flights to be guided along different approach paths, thereby increasing capacity.

At most airports either a coupled or manual ILS approach will be the norm for the sake of uniformity; other types of approach are possible, however. In good weather it is perfectly possible for a pilot to fly a completely visual approach, even without the aid of approach lighting. After all at a small club aerodrome there is no alternative! Surveillance radar approach is another option, not used in busy traffic conditions as the flight has to have the undivided attention of a controller who issues instructions by using his surveillance radar.

Lighting

With the exception of an autolanding, the pilot has to rely on the approach lighting for his final guidance on to the touchdown zone. The nearest (downwind) section of lighting is the 'line and bar' — also called Calvert line and bar after its inventor. This very clever system uses several optical principles to give the pilot very precise information on his attitude and alignment. The 'line' in the name refers to a line of bright white lights extending

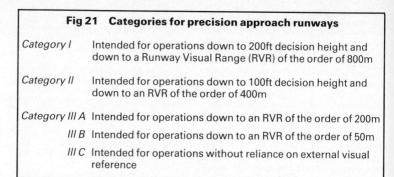

Fig 21   Categories for precision approach runways

Category I   Intended for operations down to 200ft decision height and down to a Runway Visual Range (RVR) of the order of 800m

Category II   Intended for operations down to 100ft decision height and down to an RVR of the order of 400m

Category III A   Intended for operations down to an RVR of the order of 200m

III B   Intended for operations down to an RVR of the order of 50m

III C   Intended for operations without reliance on external visual reference

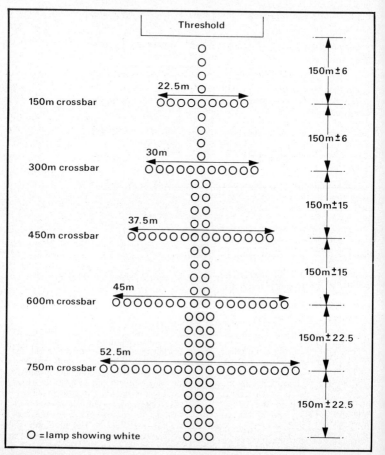

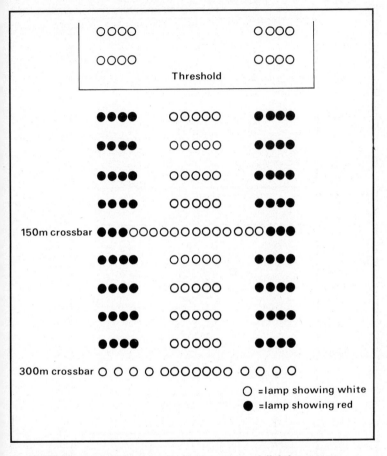

Fig 22 (left) Layout of high intensity five-bar approach lighting system applicable to Category I runways

Fig 23 (above) Supplementary lighting required within the 300m crossbar for Category II and III runways

outwards from the runway centreline; this provides a basic reference to the pilot. The width of this line reduces as the threshold is approached since the line is composed initially of three lights, then two and then one in the last 300yd. Additional red lights are fitted in this area for Category II and III operations, offering a further reference. A sequence of strobe lights is sometimes fitted along this centreline, and these flash toward the threshold indicating the landing direction.

Crossing this line are five bars of diminishing width, creating an exaggerated perspective towards the touchdown zone. These bars perform several funtions: being on a level plane they act as an artificial horizon, and they give an indication of glidescope angle. If the pilot is approaching at too gentle an angle he will

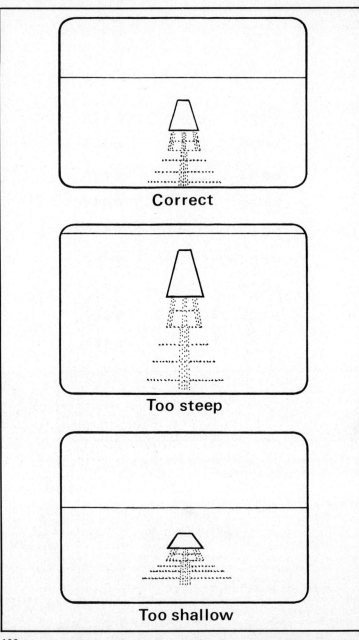

Correct

Too steep

Too shallow

Fig 24 (left) Pilot's-eye views of Line & Bar approach lighting

The famous control tower at London Heathrow Airport. At the top is the visual control room, with the ASMI head housed in the cylindrical radome above. *CAA*

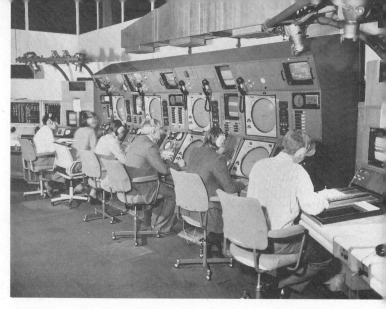

Above:
The Approach Control Room at Heathrow. *CAA*

Below:
Visual Control Room at Heathrow by night. The display to the left of the controller is that of the ASMI. The visual display units are connected to Heathrow's BASIS (British Airports Staff Information System) computer network. *CAA*

Above:
The approach lighting at Heathrow Airport. *BASL 1988*

Above right:
Closed-circuit TV camera in use at Heathrow. Such equipment is used for both security and control purposes. *Jonathan Falconer*

Below:
The departure of an Air France Boeing 747-128. The Freight Rover 'Sherpa' in the foreground is equipped as a guide vehicle; the ground engineer has just disconnected his communications lead and is signalling the aircraft to proceed around the taxiway. *Jonathan Falconer*

Above:
An ATC desk showing weather instruments on the right of the controller. *Vaisala (UK)*

Below:
Wind measurement instruments: anemometer (left) and wind vane. *Vaisala (UK)*

Below right:
Digital display for wind speed and direction, as used at ATC positions. *Vaisala (UK)*

see the pattern in a flattened form, the space between the bars closing up. Too steep an angle will lead to the pattern climbing up the flightdeck windscreen. Two further guides rely on the pilot's peripheral vision: the speed at which the bars pass beneath the aircraft indicates speed and rate of descent, and the relative movement of the two edges of the pattern reveal any deviation from the runway centreline. If all is well, the line and bar passes by in a smooth, symmetrical manner.

As a final guide to glidescope, one of two optical systems will be installed at the side of the runway: either Visual Approach Slope Indicator (VASI), or the newer Precision Approach Path Indicator (PAPI). Both use lenses and filters which produce red or white aspects when

Fig 25 Comparison of PAPI and VASI systems

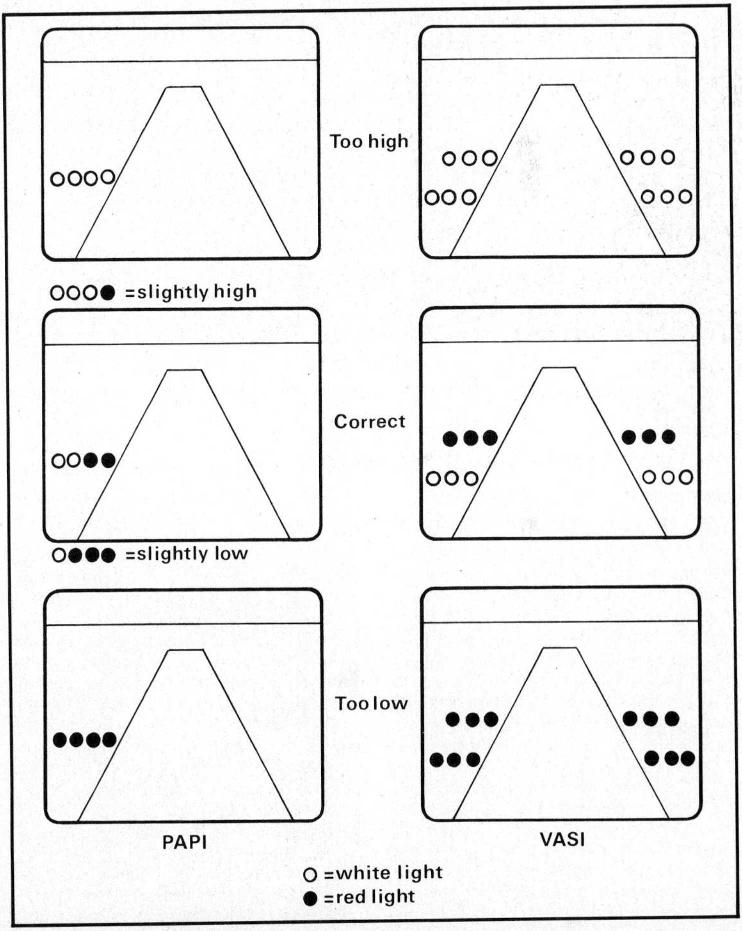

OOOO = slightly high

OO●● = slightly low

O●●● = slightly low

PAPI   VASI

O = white light
● = red light

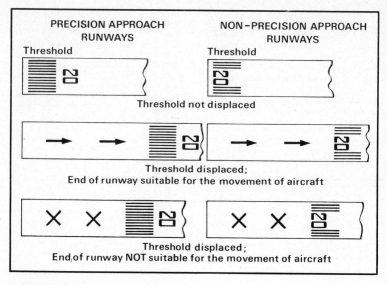

PRECISION APPROACH RUNWAYS

NON-PRECISION APPROACH RUNWAYS

Threshold

Threshold

Threshold not displaced

Threshold displaced;
End of runway suitable for the movement of aircraft

Threshold displaced;
End of runway NOT suitable for the movement of aircraft

Fig 26 Runway threshold markings

Fig 27 Runway touchdown zone markings

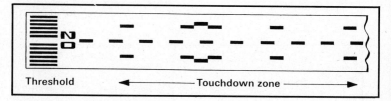

Threshold ◄──────── Touchdown zone ────────►

viewed from different angles. Because of the relative accuracy of the light units, the two systems are significantly different.

The older VASI uses two, or perhaps three, rows of lights on both sides of the runway. When seen from below the required 3° angle, both rows will display red lights; too high an approach results in all white lights. On the correct glidescope, however, the nearer row will be white and the further, red. A third row of lights is required when the runway is used by aircraft whose pilot's eye-level is more than 15ft above the level of the main wheels. In these circumstances the pilot aims for two downwind bars being white and the upwind bar showing red.

PAPI, which is to become the international standard in 1995, uses lamps which again project a beam which is vertically split between red at the bottom and white at the top. The difference from VASI lies in the sharper cut-off between the two sectors (3min of arc, against 15min for VASI). This precision allows their installation in one row of four units, each with four lamps, set at slightly increasing angles (2°30', 2°50', 3°10' and 3°30'). Thus a pilot on a correct approach will see two white and two red lights, but if he slips below the glidescope the other lights will successively show red until he is faced with a solid row of reds. Too high an approach will, conversely, result in all white lights. Because of their accuracy, PAPIs need only be installed on one side of the runway, preferably the left.

The start of the actual touchdown zone

is marked by a transverse bar of green lights, whilst the zone itself is marked by groups of white lights set into the runway surface. These have the effect of giving depth to the runway besides showing the touchdown area. Beside the touchdown zone, and down either side of the runway for its entire length, are white edge lights together with a single row of white centre lights also set into the surface. At the upwind end a bar of transverse red lights mark the limit of usable runway. These lights are all backed up by markings painted on the runway in white paint. In practice, however, the lighting system tends to be lit for the whole time, especially with intensive traffic levels.

Taxiways are subject to their own system of lights, green for centreline and blue for edge. Where a high-speed turn-off from a main runway is provided, the entrance to it is marked by the green taxiway centreline lights running parallel to the white runway centrelines for 60m before the turn. At this point they will veer off on to the taxiway. Yellow lights may be seen mixed in with the green lights on some taxiways; this is to warn pilots that they are taxiing in an area sensitive to the ILS localiser. Taxiway lighting fulfils a traffic control function at many major airports; the taxi route to be followed can be selected in the control tower, whilst red 'stop' bars across the taxiway can be lit to denote a holding point. In this way an arrival can be guided all the way from the runway to its allocated stand. Vehicles with 'follow me' and 'stop' signs on their roofs can be seen at most airports; their function is to guide aircraft through areas outside the normal taxying routes.

Besides controlling the taxiway lighting, the lighting control desk in the VCR can be used to adjust the intensity of the approach or runway lighting at the request of a pilot. The desk takes the form of a miniature plan of the airport, with switches to control the various elements. Taxying routes can be set up from the desk, which often incorporates electronic interlocks to avoid conflicting movements, similar to railway signalling.

Mention was made earlier of the accuracy required when docking an aircraft against an airbridge. Most nose-in stands have a white line painted down the centre of the stand, and there are several aids available to help guide the pilot to the correct stopping point. Most of these aids are optical devices, giving both lateral and longitudinal advice. Information on the longitudinal position of the aircraft is often given quite simply by a side marker board — ie a board fastened to the side of the terminal building, marked with white lines identified with different aircraft types. The pilot merely taxis forward until the relevant mark lines up with the flightdeck side window. Other systems rely on parallax error: the effect of objects appearing to move relative to each other when the view point changes. One system

Fig 28 Schematic representation of 'no loss' generating set

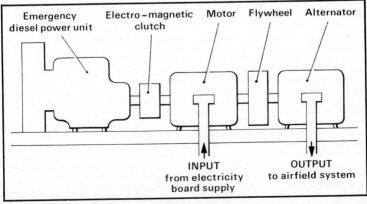

Emergency diesel power unit   Electro–magnetic clutch   Motor   Flywheel   Alternator

INPUT
from electricity
board supply

OUTPUT
to airfield system

uses a board, similar to a side marker, but with a horizontal slot cut along it. Through this slot can be seen a section of a vertical fluorescent tube, fixed further back than the board's face. As the pilot moves slowly forward, this light is seen to move along the slot until it fits in between the upper and lower marks for the aircraft type.

Lateral guidance is available from a device called Azimuth Guidance for Nose-In Stands (AGNIS), which operates in a manner not unlike PAPI. When the aircraft is centred on the stand the pilot sees two vertical green bars, but any deviation will cause the bar on the side of the error to turn red. Another guidance system uses pressure pads fastened to the stand surface to detect the position of the nosewheel. As the docking position is approached, a line of lights in front of the aircraft counts down to the correct position. Where no optical or electronic aids are available, the pilot will be directed by a ground marshaller wielding batons (illuminated at night) in the time-honoured fashion.

A series of numbers will often be seen against the stand number: this is the exact position of the stand in degrees, minutes and seconds. This is entered into the Inertial Navigation System (INS) by the pilot of a departing aircraft as a datum for the beginning of the flight. So accurate is INS that a general position for the airport is not precise enough.

All this navigation equipment must, of course, be maintained to the highest degree of accuracy and reliability. To this end, all aids are inspected from the ground on a daily basis and are regularly vetted by flying through the system and minutely checking every component. Photographs are often taken; from these, any units either not operating or out of alignment can be quickly identified. The CAA maintains its own flying unit to provide the equipment needed for the calibration and inspection of navaids, and this visits all UK airports regularly to prove the serviceability of all fittings.

Related to reliability is the supply of electric power to the airport navigation and control services: the CAA lays down very specific requirements to ensure that any interruption to supply is kept to an absolute minimum. Approach lighting for instance must relight in a second, or less, following a power failure. This reliability

can be achieved in one of two ways: an alternative supply can be routed into the airport from a totally separate section of the national grid from the primary, or a 'no loss' standby generator may be used. This second method uses a motor-alternator set coupled to a heavy flywheel to supply power under normal circumstances. In the event of a mains failure, the energy stored in the flywheel drives the alternator until a diesel engine starts and accelerates up to match the speed of the motor-alternator. An electric clutch engages at this point and the diesel then provides the motive power. Under the circumstances outlined above, the crew of an aircraft on approach would only notice a slight dimming of the lighting until the auxiliary power unit was on load.

Meteorological equipment

Various sensors for meteorological information will be seen around the airfield. The most obvious is the wind sock, still used as a 'belt and braces' display for pilots preparing to take-off. Accurate wind strength and direction data is provided by an anemometer and wind vane, respectively. The anemometer measurers wind speed by sensing the speed of rotation of a number of cups fastened to a vertical shaft, whilst the wind vane is an ordinary weather vane remotely connected to a display.

Barometric pressure is of vital concern to a pilot approaching an airport: the local pressure (QFE) is given to him by either the ATIS or approach controller and he adjusts the altimeters to this pressure so they will read zero on the runway. The instrument providing this reading is a very sophisticated barometer, often using three pressure elements, so that if one unit develops a fault the others can alert the circuitry to ignore the rogue reading.

Cloudbase data is provided by a cloud ceilometer which projects a series of laser pulses upwards. These are reflected back from the underside of the cloud, and the instrument times the pulses on their round trip. As the speed of light is known, it is theoretically easy to translate that time into a distance. When the calculations are completed in millionths of a second, however, it is obvious that theory is often a lot more simple than practice!

A final piece of information essential to the pilot is horizontal visibility, known in

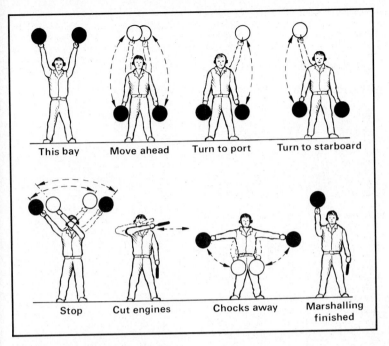

This bay	Move ahead	Turn to port	Turn to starboard
Stop	Cut engines	Chocks away	Marshalling finished

Fig 29 Ground marshalling signals

this case as Runway Visual Range (RVR). The classic method of ascertaining this reading is to sit some poor unfortunate soul in a cabin at the side of the runway. Once in the Runway Observing Position (ROP) his job is to count the number of runway edge lights that he can see and report his findings to the tower by telephone. As this duty is always carried out in foggy conditions, it is not too popular a job, especially as the regulations specify that the ROP must offer minimum resistance to a charging aircraft!

A more modern approach to RVR measurement is to use transmissometers: instruments that project a flash of light from a projector to a receiver. By comparing the known brilliance of the flash with the brilliance when it is received, the loss of light over the known distance between the two units can be computed, and the visibility — or lack of it — determined. Transmissometers are installed at either end of the runway and at the midpoint.

The displays from all these sensors are displayed at all ATC positions, and to a number of other users such as the meteorological office and emergency services. A modern trend is to display the data from all meteorological instruments together on one visual display unit, which is displayed at control positions as before but also forms a page of the airport's internal information service. In this form it can be called up by any subscriber to the system.

A final area to be loosely classed as navigation is noise monitoring. Most airports maintain automatic sound level monitors; Heathrow has 13, for example. These are remotely sited under the departure routes and, as each noise measurement is timed, any transgressor of the noise abatement procedures can be brought to book by comparing the time of the overflying to ATC records. In this way, sanctions can be taken against the operator, and complaints from the public verified.

8 Airport Maintenance

As we have seen from preceding chapters, the operation of an airport is an involved, highly technical process. The procedures outlined so far have related largely to how the airport handles its traffic, but now we take a look at an area rarely considered by the travelling public — the work which goes into keeping the actual fabric safe and capable of being used in nearly all weathers. Runways, taxiways and aprons must be maintained so as to be clear of debris, ice and snow, not only to ensure good adhesion for braking, but also to help prevent any foreign matter being sucked into aircraft engines.

Patrols

All airside areas come under the overall control of the airport's operations and safety unit, which regularly patrols the airport in vehicles, usually yellow Land Rovers. The duties of those on patrol are many and various, and their vehicles are equipped for a number of tasks; this equipment includes radios tuned to both ATC and domestic frequencies, loudspeakers and extra lighting for night patrols. Operators have a statutory duty to patrol the active area; at a busy airport this is a continual process, with patrol vehicles inspecting runways between air traffic movements. For this reason their vehicles are brightly painted and well lit, whilst the crews monitor the tower radio frequencies constantly. During their inspections the unit will be looking for such items as damage to the runway surface, unserviceable lighting and objects dropped on to the runways from either aircraft or ground vehicles. Another very important duty is bird scaring.

Birdstrike prevention

Birds present a particular hazard to modern aircraft, especially during take-off and landing, when the loss of power resulting from the ingestion of one bird or more into an engine could have catastrophic results. The treatment of the hazard begins with creating an environment which is not attractive to birds; as an example (although Gatwick airport is liberally planted with trees) emphasis is given to excluding trees which bear berries which could attract feeding birds in autumn. Similarly, land in the area beneath approach and departure routes is kept under scrutiny to ensure that bird-attracting activities such as rubbish dumping are discouraged. If the patrols spot large numbers of birds on the grass areas surrounding the runways they have several ways of discouraging them, the time-honoured method to fire a Very pistol at them. A more scientific process which is in general use these days involves identifying the type of bird involved and playing that bird's alarm call over the patrol vehicle's loudspeaker, these calls being recorded on tape cassettes carried onboard for the purpose.

Considerable success has been achieved at military airfields by the flying of birds of prey, such as sparrow-hawks over the grass areas, the results of this scare being quite long-lasting. This remedy is not available to many civil operators, however, as it can only be applied when there is no air traffic. Instead, attention is given to maintaining the grass at the length least attractive to birds. It used to be thought that very short grass was the best deterrent, but recent research has indicated that grass which is slightly longer leads to the birds feeling insecure, as they are unable to see the approach of potential predators. On the other hand, very long grass gives a home to small creatures which might attract birds as a source of food.

Grass cutting

The grass is cut, therefore, to be at the optimum length during the spring, and again in the autumn, prior to the end of the growing season. An exception to this is the strip containing the runway edge lighting, this being kept short so as not to impair the visibility of these lights. Some airports actually make a profit from their grass cutting by letting the grassed area out to farmers, who crop it for forage. Care must, of course, be taken to make sure that the personnel involved are thoroughly versed in airport safety procedures and that their machinery carries ATC radio equipment to regulate its movement about active areas. These conditions being met, the grass is harvested using standard agricultural harvesting machinery.

Runway cleaning

Whatever means is used for grass cutting, care must be taken to ensure that none of it is left blowing around waiting to be sucked into a passing jet engine. Once again, cleanliness is strictly maintained airside to prevent the risk of debris causing damage to aircraft using the field. The great volume of air entering the intake of a large turbofan engine produces a considerable gale which can pick up quite large objects and propel them into the blading, with potentially expensive or even lethal consequences. Sharp objects also pose a threat by their ability to damage undercarriage components, including tyres. For these reasons active areas are regularly and thoroughly swept, whilst 'good housekeeping' is instilled into the employees of the airport and those working for airlines and contractors; the aim is to prevent the dropping of dangerous litter such as polythene bags.

Aprons are often swept by machines very similar to those used by local authorities for road sweeping, these ranging from small, highly manoeuvrable sweepers which can operate close up to parked aircraft, to full-sized machines based on four-wheeled lorry chassis. When sweeping runways and taxiways, however, a different class of machine is called for — one which is capable of operating at far greater speed, and far more thoroughly, than a conventional road sweeper. The Lacre runway sweeper, for example, can clean at a speed of 25mph without the use of water, which is important in freezing conditions. There are two features of interest on the Lacre machine: the first is the large

mirrors mounted on long arms above the cab, which allow the driver to see any air traffic approaching from behind by looking through roof windows; and the second is the magnetic bar behind the rear wheels used for picking up any ferrous debris left by the main suction equipment.

Another cleaning task which must be regularly undertaken is the removal of rubber from the touchdown zone pavement and lighting. If left, this rubber deposited by aircraft tyres could obliterate the runway markings and become slippery in wet conditions. Several methods are in use for this task, employing chemical solvents, heat or mechanical scrubbing. The runway lighting poses a special problem as great care has to be taken not to scratch the glass lenses of the lamp units. The solution to this problem has been to use powdered walnut shells, blasted in a jet of compressed air, to scrub the rubber away; although the shells have abrasive properties, their relative softness obviates damage to the glass, thereby ensuring the optical efficiency.

Runway repairs

At most busy airports much of this work has to be carried out at night when lower levels of air traffic movements allow the closure of a runway for a time. Maintenance to the runway pavement must also, if possible, take place during these hours, requiring as it does the obstruction of runway by vehicles and equipment. The runway pavement takes terrific punishment, with very heavy loads thumping down on to it at speed, many times a day. The result is that the concrete or tarmac is liable to break up after a period of time, particularly in the area of the expansion joints. The debris produced by such damage must be regularly swept away, pending a repair being made, but repair work gives rise to problems caused by the limited time available in which to undertake it.

This time factor has led to the development of repair materials incorporating quick-setting epoxy resins, allowing repairs to be made that will cure (or go hard) very quickly. Epoxy Products, a company based in Dorset, produces a mortar which cures in as little as 30min. The damaged patch is dressed with a power tool, leaving a clean edge which is undercut to provide a key; the area is then cleaned and filled with a mixture of resin and a hardening agent. The mixture is levelled and left to harden, after which the runway can be returned to traffic. More major work is required from time to time as, eventually, the whole runway structure will need replacing. This work is carried out in sections to minimise the length of time that the runway is inoperative. Coming between these extremes of maintenance is work needed occasionally to restore a runway's friction characteristics; this task normally entails scoring the pavement surface with power-driven diamond cutting wheels.

The subject of runway friction is one which exercises the minds of airport operators to a considerable extent. The obvious result of reduced friction is the increase in the braking distance of aircraft using the runway, but the effects go beyond this. The electronic automatic braking and spoiler systems fitted to modern aircraft rely on the rapid acceleration to full speed of the main wheels. This acceleration is accompanied by much smoke and screeching on a dry runway but, in slippery conditions, problems can arise; some method must, therefore, be used to alert aircrew of prevailing runway conditions.

Several methods for assessing runway friction exist, ranging from static testing to the use of high-speed monitoring units. A common device is the Mu Meter — mu (μ) being a Greek symbol assigned to the coefficient of friction. This device resembles a three-wheeled trailer which is towed behind a runway patrol vehicle, and interprets the castoring force generated by two smooth-tyred wheels which are held in a 'toed out' configuration (ie, one where the wheels are not parallel to each other, but point outwards). This force is proportional to the runway friction, so this can be continually assessed and transmitted to the tower. From there this information is relayed to aircraft preparing to use the airport.

Other friction-assessing devices detect the tension in a chain-drive coupling wheels which revolve at slightly different speeds. Once again, this tension is proportional to the friction under the wheels. The Saab surface friction tester is an example of this type, but from the outside it resembles a standard Saab coupé. Under the skin, however, is a fifth

wheel coupled to the rear axle, and it is the tension in the drive between them that equates with the friction. The Saab unit can incorporate a water tank which wets the runway to a uniform depth; this method is used to calibrate a newly-surfaced runway for future reference. From then on routine runs are used, during wet or icy conditions, to determine the condition of the runway, or part of it.

Winter operations

Snow and ice are the conditions most likely to cause severe loss of friction. Snow has other attributes which render flying operations hazardous; drag on the wheels can cause a loss of acceleration on take-off, whilst any snow or slush ingested into engines could cause serious damage. All UK airports hold a large selection of equipment in readiness for these winter conditions, along with staff trained in their use. Some airports use RFFS personnel to man their machines whilst others take drivers from other duties. All this equipment is thoroughly serviced during the summer so as to be on stand-by from the end of autumn.

During winter the weather forecast gives the first alert of impending freezing conditions, whilst airfield meteorological equipment such as ice detectors and humidity sensors give more immediate warnings of danger. The first line of defence against ice is the spreading of anti-icer, both solid and liquid chemicals being used for the purpose. The requirements are for an anti-icer which is non-toxic and incapable of causing corrosion damage to an aircraft or its components. For these reasons salt is unsuitable and so is sand because of its abrasive properties.

The liquids used are often based on glyco-ethylene, but suffer from the disadvantages of high cost coupled with causing initial slippery conditions before actually melting ice. When liquids are used they are spread from a road tanker either fitted with spray bars or hydraulically-driven spinners which throw the liquid in a circular pattern. The most common solid anti-icer in use is urea, an organic compound. This is supplied in granular — or prilled — form and is dispensed from spreaders similar in appearance to highway gritters. These machines deliver the urea from a large

Top:
The Lacre runway sweeper is based on a Bedford 'TL' chassis. This unit is capable of sweeping a runway thoroughly at 25mph, and is much quicker than a highway sweeper The mirrors above the cab provide the driver with a view to the rear of the vehicle; also interesting is the bar behind the rear wheels which contains magnets to remove ferrous debris from the runway. *Lacre*

Above:
The Fricomer runway sweeper fitted with snow broom for winter use. When working as a sweeper, the brooms between the wheels are swung out to create a wide sweep pattern. *Author*

119

Above left:
This urea spreader is mounted on a Bedford 'M' type chassis. *Author*

Left and below left:
The Weiser multi de-icer is capable of spreading both solid and liquid media. *Rolba*

Above:
Snow broom equipment mounted on Mercedes-Unimog 4×4 chassis. *Author*

Below:
Schorling snow broom, showing the brush and centrifugal fan and blower nozzles.
Author

Above:
The Rolba 'Super Sweeper' in action. *Rolba*

Below:
Luton Airport's snowplough line-up, comprising Magirus-Deutz and Bedford vehicles.
Author

Bottom:
A close-up of the Magirus-Deutz 4×4 snowplough tender, towing a snow broom unit.
Author

Above:
The Rolba R1000 snow blower: the blades at the front cut the snow and throw it back into the large impeller immediately behind. The impeller throws the powdered snow through the chute visible to the right of the cab.   *Author*

Below:
A Rolba R400 snow blower, similar in principle to the previous machine, but with a smaller output.   *Author*

Above:
The snow shovel is used for apron work, the example here is mounted on a
Massey-Ferguson 4×4 tractor. *Author*

Below:
Similar equipment is carried here by a County 4×4 tractor at Heathrow. These tractors
can also be fitted with powerful winches for aircraft recovery duty. *County Tractors*

hopper by means either of a belt or an arger, and on to a spinner which flings it over a wide area. Some machines incorporate long booms which convey the granules out to spinners mounted at the outer ends, thereby producing an even wider spread pattern. Most spreaders built for airport work use a system which wets the urea as it is applied; in dry conditions, this sticks the granules to the surface long enough for them to start acting.

If snow and ice are forecast, the aim is to treat the runways, taxiways and aprons before the event. Neighbouring airfields, both civil and military, co-operate by informing one another of the approach of snow conditions thereby allowing a thorough application of anti-icer immediately before the fall. This ensures that snow falls on to a wet surface, prolonging the time taken for it to settle and rendering it easier to clear once it has. Once settling starts, however, mechanical means must be used to clear the snow.

At the same time, air traffic control will be feeding data into the national and international ATC system about conditions at their field. This is achieved by completing an internationally uniform document called a SNOWTAM, which includes all relevant information on runway state, height of snowbanks and likely outlook. This data is coded in a standard format and transmitted by the ATC telex system where it becomes part of the pre-flight briefing for pilots. They all use this information to make decisions on fuel loads, landing weights and so on, therefore frequent updates to the SNOW-TAM are necessary.

Meanwhile, back out on the airport once snow has begun to settle, the first process is the use of snow brooms. These are large revolving brushes, either mounted on a self-propelled chassis or a trailer. This brush, which is adjustable so as to sweep to either side of the unit, is hydraulically-powered by a diesel engine which also provides the power for a large fan. The air from this fan is fed to a nozzle capable of blowing loose snow from the runway surface after the passage of the brush. The snow brooms operate in teams, driving along the runway in a diagonal line, each broom — if not self-propelled — being towed behind a snowplough. The brush of each broom unit is angled so as to discharge down-

wind, and into the path of the following unit. In this way the snow is swept from broom to broom until it is cast clear of the downwind side of the runway.

When the snowfall becomes heavier the brooms will be overwhelmed, so the blades of the snow ploughs will be brought into action. The carrying vehicles are invariably tough, all-wheel drive vehicles, often with a military or construction industry origin. In the recent past, Bedford 'RL' and 'M' types have been popular — indeed, many are still to be seen — but a more powerful vehicle in the shape of the IVECO (Magirus Deutz) is now finding as much favour in Britain as in its native West Germany. This normal control vehicle, either 4×4 or 6×6, employs an air-cooled Deutz diesel engine which removes the problem of freezing up from the operator's mind.

The snow plough blade itself is a massive item, far bigger than anything used for highway clearing. The angle of the blade is adjustable to allow snow to be thrown to either side of the vehicle, again into the path of the following unit; the snow broom still being used to complete the operation. The bottom edge of the blade itself is fitted with replaceable rubber sections which serve to protect the runway lighting and markings from the damage that steel would inflict.

After several passes of the snow plough line, a sizeable bank of snow will have accumulated at the runway edge. If left, this would not only obscure the edge lighting, but would be liable to ingestion into aircraft engines; consequently these banks must be removed. The machine to perform this task is called a snow blower, or a rotary snow plough. This uses a large helical cutter, mounted across the front of the vehicle, to pick up and break up the snow and throw it back into the centre of a high speed, centrifugal impeller which is mounted behind it. The impeller propels the snow out of a chute and casts it downwind on to the grass, well clear of the runway.

A typical machine is the Rolba R1000, built in Switzerland like so much winter maintenance equipment. This is powered by a Volvo diesel engine of 317bhp which drives the blower head via a four-speed gearbox, the road wheels being driven by an infinitely-variable hydrostatic transmission. This latter enables forward speed to be adjusted to exactly the

Fig 30 Method employed for clearing snow from runways

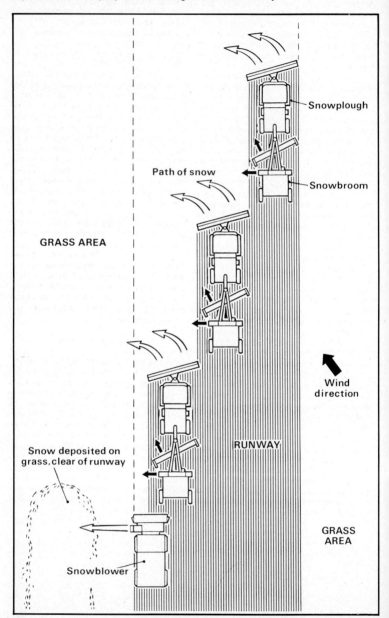

Snowplough

Path of snow

Snowbroom

GRASS AREA

Wind direction

Snow deposited on grass, clear of runway

RUNWAY

GRASS AREA

Snowblower

optimum for efficiency. The machine is capable of clearing up to 2,500 tonnes of snow per hour at speeds of up to 18mph. Considering that a 4in fall of snow at Heathrow requires the shifting of about 75,000 tonnes of the stuff to remain in operation, such performance comes in handy!

There is a problem with using such machines in Britain, however, and that involves the quality of the snow which falls here. Television pictures often show these units at work in the Alps, prompting questions as to why we do not make more extensive use of them in the UK. The snow encountered in central Europe is light and powdery after its long track over the land, making it relatively easy to handle; in Britain, with nowhere any great distance from the sea, the snow is wet and heavy. These qualities greatly reduce the efficiency of any snow-handling machinery, a fact often overlooked by some in their annual criticism of winter preparations.

Apron areas also need clearing, but the need for speed is not quite as great as that for runways and taxiways. Large agricultural-type 4×4 tractors are frequently utilised with very large snow shovels mounted in front to bulldoze the snow to the edge of the apron; from here it is removed by power-loader and lorry. An alternative is to use powered brushes, smaller than the snow brooms already described, driven by the tractor's power take-off. Similar equipment can be mounted on runway sweepers, which obviously cannot perform their primary duty when snow is on the ground.

Rather than remove snow, much thought is devoted to lessening its effect in the first place. The use of light, frangible fencing, placed some distance back from runways and taxiways, can start the formation of snowbanks which serve to protect active areas during blizzard conditions. Judicially placed, these fences can repay their cost many times over by preventing the build of snow on the downwind side of them. Plastic fencing originally developed for providing shelter to upland sheep is now used, after winter it is merely rolled up and stored to facilitate grass cutting.

Aircraft recovery

A final nightmare facing all airport operators is that involving a heavy aircraft leaving the runway strip and becoming bogged down. Various methods can be used to effect recovery in such a situation, all revolving around the need to spread the aircraft's weight over as wide an area as possible. Supplies of metal matting are usually kept to hand, and these are linked together to form a temporary roadway from the site to the taxiway. Trolleys are placed under the aircraft's strongpoints and jacks or airbags used to transfer weight from the undercarriage to the trolleys. The whole assemblage is then winched back on to firm ground and lowered back on to the aircraft's own wheels. At a greater level of sophistication is the use of modular hover-pallets, which are fastened together to form a large raft supported by an air cushion. This spreads the weight over a very large area of ground without the use of any form of roadway.

This chapter has dwelt on the problems faced by the operator in keeping the airport operational, often in spite of the worst that the weather can do. Much of the equipment used is highly specialised and therefore very costly. The fact that this equipment is provided, often by statute, illustrates the absolute importance attached to the safety of their air traveller and, indeed, the public in general. Every eventuality is guarded against, experience dictating modifications to machinery and practices, following the theme of the entire safety philosophy of UK airport operators.

Glossary

ac	alternating current
AFTN	Aeronautical Fixed Telecommunications Network
AGNIS	Azimuth Guidance-Nose In Stands
Airside	The area of an airport devoted to aviation, thus inside security and customs controls
APU	Auxiliary Power Unit
ASMI	Airfield Surface Movement Indicator
ATC	Air Traffic Control
ATCC	Air Traffic Control Centre
ATIS	Automated Terminal Information Service
ATM	Air Traffic Movement
ATN	Administrative Telephone Network
AVGAS	Aviation gasoline
AVTUR	Aviation turbine fuel
CAA	Civil Aviation Authority
C of A	Certificate of Airworthiness
dc	direct current
DFTI	Distance From Touchdown Indicator
DRDF	Digital Resolution Direction Finder
FAA	Federal Aviation Administration
GPU	Ground Power Unit
ICAO	International Civil Aviation Organisation
ILS	Instrument Landing System
LAFB	Local Authority Fire Brigade
Landside	The area of an airport not concerned with aviation, to which the public have unrestricted access
LFT	Light Foam Tender
MFT	Major Foam Tender
MTI	Moving Target Indicator
NATS	National Air Traffic Services
NDB	Non-Directional Beacon
Notam	Notice to airmen
PAPI	Precision Approach Path Indicator
PTO	Power take-off (from a road vehicle's engine)
QFE	Barometric pressure at aerodrome level
QNH	Barometric pressure at sea level
RFFS	Rescue and Fire Fighting Service
RIV	Rapid Intervention Vehicle
ROP	Runway Observing Position
RT	Radio Telephone
RVP	Rendezvous Point
RVR	Runway Visual Range
SID	Standard Instrument Departure
SSR	Secondary Surveillance Radar
STAR	Standard Arrival Route
STOL	Short Take-off and Landing
UHF	Ultra High Frequency
VASI	Visual Approach Slope Indicator
VCR	Visual Control Room
VHF	Very High Frequency
VOR	VHF Omnidirectional Radio Range (Beacon)
VTOL	Vertical Take-off and Landing